D0916564

Praise for
By Her Side

"While eating disorders take some of our loved ones away, there are many who find full recovery and live. This beautifully written book explores both of these pathways: grief and then healing from tragedy and the joy of full recovery from illness."

—Michael E. Berrett, PhD
Psychologist, CEO and Co-founder of Center for Change
Co-author of *Spiritual Approaches in the Treatment of Women with Eating Disorders*

"Our society praises those that are able to lose weight and be skinny. What we don't always realize is the emotional and physical damage that can come from solely focusing on size as a determinant for internal health and external beauty. *By Her Side* is a way to show people the intense struggle of an eating disorder and to begin to help us change the way we view health and beauty."

—Kathy Spencer MS, CHES

"As a physician who has spent half my career caring for these wonderful, yet complex patients, I am grateful that *By Her Side* sheds much-needed light on the this often misunderstood world of eating disorders. In a society that spends billions to improve body image, perhaps no other generation has grown up more inundated with daily images of false, photo-shopped bodily perfection than today. Just as extreme as this plague of unattainable physical perfection has become, so has this equally extreme but dark plague silently affecting millions of women and men. Unable to accept their own bodies as they are, these prisoners of their eating disorders have embarked on a lonely war against food and against themselves—slowly and quietly killing themselves, seeking a false prize that is perpetually "just five more pounds" away. You know them. They might be your mother, your sister, your best friend, your roommate, your brother or your neighbor. There is hope! There is help! Recovery is possible! For someone you know, however, time might be running out."

—Steven L. Berry, M.D., Family Practice Physician

by her side

by her side

DEBORAH P. SCHONE &
SHELBY L. EVANS LSUDC

Published by Familius LLC, www.familius.com

Familius books are available at special discounts for bulk purchases for sales promotions, family, or corporate use. Special editions, including personalized covers, excerpts of existing books, or books with corporate logos, can be created in large quantities for special needs. For more information, contact Premium Sales at 559-876-2170 or email special-markets@familius.com

Library of Congress Catalog-in-Publication Data

2014941301

pISBN 978-1-938301-96-4

eISBN 978-1-938301-65-0

Printed in the United States of America

Edited by Aimee Hancock

Cover Design by David Miles

Book Design by Maggie Wickes

10 9 8 7 6 5 4 3 2 1

First Edition

for Kristin

LET'S STAY FRIENDS

I shed a tear the day you left; I thought I never would heal.
Those crazy feelings inside me burn.
Don't say my love wasn't real.
You were all I had, the one who kept me living.
My first love of many, you kept me believing.
How can I stand here and say goodbye, when I know it's the end?
There is one thing I want, oh, so much,
"Let's stay friends, Let's stay friends"

I'll always cherish the time we spent
And all those warm memories.
When I look back through times in life,
Oh, baby, what will I see?
A best friend who cared.
Who fought with me through hardship?
Who carried me up high, who knows where my heart is?
Where can I turn to, to hide the hurt?
I still love deep down inside.
My broken heart will never mend.
"Let's stay friends, please let's stay friends."

Why do the times go, oh so fast?
I was always told love was meant to last,
Yet when that time comes, you must let go,
But that friendship should always grow.

I cared so much, my pain was real.
Please suspend me in time.
She's gone forever, but at least I know she was mine.
She was mine.
It's the end.
But, please, "Let's stay friends."

—Holly Stone, May 1986
"A song of friendship for our Kris"

acknowledgments

We would like to express a special thanks and sincere appreciation to all those who believed in *By Her Side*. We received help and encouragement along the way from many people, which made telling this story and raising awareness of eating disorders possible.

Deborah would like to thank her husband Steve and her children Skylar, Hunter, Hannah, Kenya, Noah, Anwar, Luke, Emma, and Zak. She would also like to thank the following people for their support and valuable contributions to the book: Nicole Hadley, Robert and Catherine Pedersen, Amanda Jensen, Mark O. Haroldsen, Lois Haroldsen, Mark E. Haroldsen, Nicky Haroldsen, David Haroldsen, Cammy Haroldsen, Marcus Haroldsen, George Poulton, Lindsey Poulton Machan, Stephanie Read Wickens, Marcy Liljenquist Benson, Michele Wilson Cunningham, Rosemary Murdoch Thomas, Holly S., Wendy, Alacyn, Amy, Kia, Tracy, Kathy, Kimberlee, Kathy Lenette, Heather, Jenny, Janette, Monica, and Holly C.

Shelby would like to thank her husband, Kenny, for his loving support and encouragement, as well as her daughter, Brooklyn. She would also like to thank the following people for their help and continued support along this journey: Arlin and Leslie Satterthwaite, Wilford and Louise Evans, Iann Johnson, Stacy Beatty, Shane Holmes, and all of the individuals who participated in the Beautiful Survey for providing honest and sincere responses.

Furthermore, thanks to Dr. Michael Berrett, PhD, for sharing his wisdom, knowledge, and expertise in the area of mental health and eating disorders. His insight has proven to be most valuable and we appreciate the time and effort he spent to help us fine tune *By Her Side*.

The true gems of *By Her Side* are Kristin Haroldsen and Becky Berry. Without their stories, this book would not have been possible. We would like to thank Kristin for being who she was and touching so many lives in her short time on earth. We would like to thank Becky for being a beacon of light and a true inspiration to those who are struggling to find their path to recovery.

contents

foreword

First and foremost, I express my heartfelt sympathy and compassion for co-author Deborah Schone, friends, and family members, all of whom suffered the monumental loss of this precious young woman, Kristin Haroldsen. She died because of her eating disorder. I express gratitude for the willingness of each individual to peel back the covers of memory and share their thoughts, feelings, and experiences so that all who become aware of this story might receive the benefit of their suffering, their work, and their courageous sharing. Their loss can become—for the reader and all who become acquainted with this story—the seedbed of awareness and understanding, of a desire to accept and help those suffering, and of the resolve for efforts toward prevention and treatment. Despite this tragic loss, the overarching message of this book is that eating disorders are treatable and that, for most who seek and remain in the saddle of treatment, the hope for full recovery is real.

I honor coauthor Shelby Evans for her ten years of hard and effective work and leadership in the trenches of direct patient care in an in-patient and residential treatment program. This book reflects understanding which comes only from living in the world with those who are suffering and from seeing firsthand, and repeatedly, what works and what doesn't work in efforts to transcend illness. Additionally, Shelby's training as a substance abuse counselor has given her invaluable insight, which is an education and blessing to those suffering illness, their families, and professionals alike. Shelby looks at eating disorder illness through the lens of the addictive process, and this unique perspective is valuable in understanding illness and in efforts to help those suffering.

Becky Berry, a significant contributor to this book, has walked the lonely, lengthy, painful path from the form of a skeleton and the inner life of torment and fear to the respite of full recovery from her eating disorder illness. She has transcended illness and created a life of joy, love, relationships, healing, and freedom from the iron clasp of a hellish illness, difficult but possible to beat. She has shared her experience and pathway to recovery, including the powerful and healing role that faith and spirituality played in her journey. Becky is an amazing woman who has faced fear, defied illness, and now lights up any room she enters. She is another special example that recovery is real and that joy and peace is available to us all.

This book gives a delightful offering. It teaches that (1) these illnesses must be taken seriously—they diminish the mental, emotional, and spiritual presence of a loved one and sometimes take away life itself; (2) through strength, mutual support, faith, resilience, and courage, families and friends can heal from loss, and through that loss, can make a significant contribution to individual lives and the world; (3) through study and effort, we all can increase our understanding of eating disorder illnesses, what they are, how they develop, and how we can give support, intervene, and treat them; and (4) there is important learning to be had not only from stories of loss but also from shared stories of transcendence, healing, and true recovery.

This book will take you on an intimate journey into the real lives and the dark corners of those suffering with eating disorders, and the lives of those who stand by them and love them. It will open eyes, pull on heart strings, illuminate understanding, raise questions which must be answered, and inspire the reader through the stories of good people suffering adversity and then finding an increase in solace, peace, and meaning. It teaches us that it is never too late to increase our understanding and that fully embracing hope is not only possible, but wise. It is an honor to have been asked to write the foreword to this book. It is a humble offering by good people whose teachings are relevant and whose lives are worthy of emulation. This book is a great contribution to the written works about eating disorders, love, and the resilience of the human soul.

Michael E. Berrett, PhD

Psychologist, CEO, and Cofounder for Center for Change

Coauthor of Spiritual Approaches in the Treatment of Women with Eating Disorders

introduction

By Her Side provides an intimate look at the reality of eating disorders and the many lives that are impacted by such illnesses. The story of Kristin Haroldsen's life and death—as a result of her eating disorder—is told from the perspective of her best friend, Deborah P. Schone. Deborah walks the reader through their friendship as she sheds light on Kristin's very likeable and outgoing personality. Kristin's influence touched many people and left them saddened and heartbroken when she died at a young age.

In part one of *By Her Side*, the reader will hear from Deborah along with Kristin's closest family members and friends including her mother, father, siblings, and best friends from high school. Each of them openly shares what it was like to learn of Kristin's condition and anxiously wait in the hospital where Kristin lay fighting for her life. With loved ones nearby, Kristin unexpectedly passes away with her mother, father, and Deborah *by her side*.

Kristin's death impacted their lives forever. Their accounts of this tragic event share how they felt in those moments, what they did in the days following her passing, and how they have managed to cope with this terrible loss over the years.

Part two of *By Her Side* is written by Shelby L. Evans, LSUDC. Shelby has ten years of experience working in the mental health field with women who struggle with eating disorders and other addictions. She has witnessed firsthand the impact that eating disorders have on women and their loved ones, and what it is like for them to seek help, embark on the road to recovery, and find healing through therapeutic interventions.

The chapters included in this section of the book will provide the reader with basic knowledge and awareness of eating disorders, including the different types of eating disorders and the behaviors associated with them, possible reasons why people engage in eating disorder behaviors, ways to establish and utilize positive coping skills, and the ideas and opinions people have regarding beauty and perceptions of body image.

The final chapter of *By Her Side* introduces Becky Berry. Becky is a young woman who has walked down the dark path entrenched in an eating disorder. Through her faith, and with the help of an interdisciplinary treatment approach, Becky was able to break free from the cycle of addiction. Here she shares the impact her eating disorder behaviors had on her life and the difficult reality of letting go of control. She walks the reader down her path to recovery and willingly shares what she has learned as a result of her battle with "Ed" (eating disorders). Becky has fully enjoyed life and the many blessings that come from choosing recovery. Her desire is to help those who continue to struggle with this illness and offer hope that recovery is possible.

prologue

Two hours had passed since arriving at the hospital; everything seemed to be playing out in slow motion.

The last time I was with Kris, I was standing a little bit away from her, almost studying the room and every detail around me. Lois came in and went right over to Kris. She picked up Kris's hand and placed it in hers and sat next to her on the bed. The room was completely silent besides the machines. Mark came into the ICU room. He had been visiting with the doctors. The doctors had told him that they should probably start to make arrangements to turn off the machines. I don't think he even realized I was there. I have tried many times to explain the expression of sadness that he had on his face, but I can never find the right words to describe it.

He said in a quiet, tender voice, "It is time, Lois. We need to start making arrangements."

Lois just stared at Kris, and then said back to Mark, "Let's make the arrangements."

PART 1

Kristin

CHAPTER 1

baking soda

May 1, 1986

It was about 9:00 p.m. and darker than usual outside. My sister Amy and I had just returned home from an aerobics class. A friend of mine told me that Sean, the boy I had asked to the upcoming girl's preference dance, was going to answer me that night.

The doorbell rang, and I ran down to the front door with excitement. There was a big "Yes" on a cake with a bunch of balloons. I picked it all up and started taking them to my room when the doorbell rang once again. I thought it was Sean coming back.

I ran back to the front door and was immediately surprised to see my best friend Kristin's (whom I knew as Kris) father, Mark. He was really angry and started yelling at me. As a sixteen-year-old girl, I was scared and I couldn't understand why he was so mad. I have always really liked her dad, and I always thought of him as fun and having a great sense of humor. He intimidated me then; I started to cry and to back away from him, trying so hard to figure out what he was saying to me—everything was happening so fast.

He proceeded to tell me, in an angry voice, that Kris was in the hospital. And he wanted to know why I hadn't told him that Kris was bulimic.

Bulimic? What does that mean? I didn't know anything about bulimia. I *did* know that my friend made herself throw up after she ate, but I didn't know that it had a name. No one ever talked about eating disorders around me.

At that moment, I couldn't comprehend why she was in the hospital and what could have happened to her. I had just been with her earlier in the day.

After school, we met Kris's mom, Lois, out in front of the high school to use the car for the afternoon. We dropped Lois off at home and then stopped at a local fast food place to get some food. As usual, we ordered hamburgers, fries, and Diet Cokes. We then went into the restaurant bathroom together, where the toilet and sink were all in the same room. I would usually look in the mirror, fixing my hair, while she leaned over the toilet, sticking her finger down the back of her throat to force herself to throw up. As weird as it may sound, I never thought that much about it. It was just what she did. I always thought it was really gross, and I didn't understand why she would want to do it, but I never thought it was wrong.

After the restaurant, she dropped me off at my house, and, as usual, when I got out of the car, I said to her, "See ya, Kris. Love ya." She always said the same thing back to me: "See ya. Love you, too."

I said, "No, Kris, I really love you."

She laughed and said, "Love you, too, kid." She often called me that. "Now get out of my car." We both laughed.

She told me that she needed to go home for dinner and she'd call me later. I got out of the car and started walking toward the front door. Right before I turned the door handle to walk inside, I turned around and watched her drive away.

Little did I know that that would be the last time I would ever see her alive.

My parents had heard Mark yelling from their bedroom and came running. My dad got in between Mark and me, trying to understand what he was saying to me. Mark blamed me for Kris being in the hospital. He blamed me for not telling him that she was making herself throw up. I wanted the yelling to stop.

It was a lot to take in, and at this point I was crying pretty hard. Mark didn't seem to care. I told him I wanted to go to the hospital to see her. He gave me a stern "No" that meant I couldn't go tonight, but that I would be able to go see her tomorrow.

My dad asked Mark to sit down and tell us exactly what had happened. We could tell Mark was still piecing everything together himself. By now, my mom joined us on the couch to hear the story.

After Kris dropped me off, she went home to have dinner with her family. Lois had brought home chicken and a couple of individual strawberry pies from a local fast food chain. Kris's parents were divorced and had been since she was thirteen. The kids were at her mom's house on this night.

When Kris finished her dinner, she excused herself from the table and ran upstairs to start on her homework before The Cosby Show *started. Lois went into the backyard with Kris's brother David.*

Kris went into her bathroom and tried to throw up her dinner so that she could start on her homework. She tried sticking her finger down the back of her throat, but, when that didn't work, she used her toothbrush in place of her finger. No matter what she did, she couldn't throw up and started to get extremely frustrated with herself.

She pulled out a box of baking soda that she kept under her bathroom sink. She had seen it used once in a movie to induce vomiting.

Kris filled a glass of water and dumped the baking soda in the glass and drank it. Later, when her mom asked how much baking soda she used, she replied, "I just took the box and dumped it."

Kris was in immediate pain. Her stomach started to hurt and burn. She held her abdomen and hunched over, screaming for her mom. Lois heard her yelling from the backyard and ran upstairs to her bedroom as fast as she could.

As soon as Lois saw her hunched over, she panicked and said, "Oh, Kris, what have you done?"

Kris told her mom what had happened and just kept saying, "I'm so sorry," over and over again. Lois helped her down the stairs and into the car. Lois assumed that she would just need her stomach pumped and thought the local health clinic would be the closest and quickest place to go. It was 6:30 p.m.

By the time they got to the clinic, Kris couldn't walk. Her stomach had bloated so much that a nurse took one look at her and said, "Are you sure she isn't pregnant?" Lois and Kris looked at each other and laughed.

They told Lois they couldn't do anything for her and that she needed to go straight to the local hospital. The nurse called ahead to make sure the hospital would be expecting them. When they arrived, the admitting nurse immediately put a needle in Kris's stomach to release some of the gases. They prepped her for surgery, and again Kris just kept saying, "I'm so sorry; I won't do it again." Lois told her she loved her and that everything would be OK. Kris was wheeled away.

What I was hearing from Mark was unbelievable. Could this be true? Could this have really happened? How could a beautiful, blonde, sixteen-year-old girl—my best friend—be in the hospital for something as little as making herself throw up? I didn't think it was that big of a deal. Was any of this my fault? At this point Mark thought she would be OK. They would pump her stomach, and she would just go home.

He started to calm down, but you could feel his sadness and anger; he needed someone to blame for what was happening. He figured I knew what she was doing since we were together all of the time, and he blamed me for not telling him. I think he was still trying to wrap his brain around all of it; it was a lot to take in. My dad finished talking to him while I just sat there, and then he left.

I remember sitting there feeling completely numb, not being able to move, and feeling emotionally drained and sad. I wanted to get in my car and go see Kris immediately. I was so angry and upset that Mark told me I couldn't go. I felt helpless, and I didn't know what to do.

My mom and dad stayed with me to make sure I was OK. They too were just finding out that Kris had this eating disorder and were confused that I hadn't mentioned anything to them before tonight. They didn't say much to me; they just tried to comfort me. I don't think they knew what to say. My mom said she'd love to go with me in the morning to see Kris.

I told them that I knew it was late, but I really wanted to go tell our other friends. I felt like I needed to be with them. They weren't thrilled about the idea of me leaving as upset as I was, but they knew it was important for me to go.

I drove straight to Stephanie's house, knocked on her bedroom window and climbed in. I started crying all over again and shared with her all the events of the evening. It was really nice to be able to talk to her. After talking to her, we went over to Marcy's house to tell her. I knew I needed to hurry because my parents would be worried about me and were probably waiting up until I got home.

Kris, Marcy, Steph, and I called ourselves the Kids of America and The Friends. We gave ourselves the name the Kids of America from a song on the radio that we would always sing in the car on our way to lunch. It became our song, but there were a lot of other girls in that group, so we came up with the name The Friends for just the four of us. We had business cards made up just for fun with our phone numbers on them so if we met someone that wanted our phone number, we would just give them one of our business cards.

Stephanie and I stayed at Marcy's only long enough to tell her what was going on. I was exhausted, to say the least, and my eyes were swollen. I needed to get some rest so that I could go see Kris in the morning. I dropped Stephanie off at her house on my way home.

My dad had waited up for me and asked how I was doing. I'm pretty sure that my appearance spoke for itself. He told me to plan on sleeping in for a little bit in the morning and then Mom would go with me to the hospital.

When I finally got in bed, I lay there for a long time, unable to sleep. I had so much on my mind that it wouldn't shut off. It must have been close to 3:00 or 4:00 a.m. when I finally fell asleep.

May 2, 1986

It was 8:05 a.m. when my big, brass doorknob hit the wall with a loud bang and woke me up. My mom was standing by my bed telling me in a hurried voice that Lois had just called—she didn't think that Kris was going to make it.

She told me we needed to go to the hospital immediately. I don't remember getting out of bed or dressing; I just remember driving to the hospital with my mom. I told her that I didn't want to go without Marcy and Stephanie. She agreed to stop by the high school and grab them. We pulled up right in front; I hopped out while she waited. I ran into the school, frantically running through the halls looking for them. I don't remember who I saw or talked to. I just remember how relieved I was when I finally found Stephanie. By then my heart was racing. I was ready to head to the hospital even though we hadn't found Marcy. My mind was blurry and I couldn't run fast enough back to the car. Stephanie and I decided just to go and others would continue to look for Marcy.

I felt like my mom was driving so slow, hitting every red light. A minute seemed like an hour. I was crying so hard, praying Kris wouldn't die.

We finally made it to the hospital and parked. We ran through the first set of automatic doors and went up the elevator. The elevator doors opened and you could see Lois at the end of the hall. She was a complete mess.

Lois was like a second mom to me and had always treated me like a daughter. She has a loving heart and is always so kind and nice to everyone. She grabbed me by the arm and said, "Let's go see her together." I asked my mom to go with us. Because Kris was in the ICU, only a few of us could go in at a time.

As I entered the room, I could see her lying in the bed. She looked awful: her stomach was bloated, her legs were black and blue, her body was swollen, and she had tubes everywhere. I only recognized her because I knew her so well. She had acrylic nails on (two of which were broken) and half her nail polish was coming off her toenails.

It was hard for me to be in there with her because it didn't look like her. I gave her swollen face a kiss. I wanted her to sit up and say, "Hey, kid."

I wanted my Kris back.

I left the room so other family members could go in and see her. In the short time of arriving at the hospital and going into the ICU, well over thirty friends from the high school had arrived to see what was going on. I don't think anyone at this point thought she would die. The halls were lined with friends, and every few minutes, more visitors would file off the elevator. Her church leaders, classmates, friends, and family were all there. The outpouring of love and support in such a short period of time was amazing to everyone.

The family was in a private room just down the hall from where Kris was. Kris was the second child of five kids at the time. She had two brothers and two sisters. I went into the room where her family was waiting. As I walked in, everyone greeted me with warmth and love. It was very quiet and somber; everyone was crying.

Mark was sitting in the corner, quiet and broken. The man that came to my home the night before was not the same man sitting in that corner now. He stood up and gave me a big hug. Not many words were exchanged. I loved her family and felt comfortable around them. It was really hard for me to see her sisters so sad and confused as to what was happening. Kris's stepsister, Lindsey, was only three, and she was holding a pink My Little Pony toy and talking to it, telling the pony that Kris was going to be OK.

I kept going back and forth between the ICU and the family's room. I talked to Kris and told her to wake up. I was mad and begged her not to die. Her eyes were closed and you could hear the breathing from the machines keeping her alive. The room was cold and I felt alone, even though she was in there with me.

I continued to go in and out, visiting Kris and talking with friends that lined the halls. It was getting out of control, and the noise level was very disruptive to other patients. Finally, the halls became so full that the hospital staff asked everyone to go down to the main floor waiting area or out to the front grass. Only family could stay on the floor.

Two hours had passed since arriving at the hospital; everything seemed to be playing out in slow motion.

The last time I was with Kris, I was standing a little bit away from her, almost studying the room and every detail around me. Lois came in and went right over to Kris. She picked up Kris's hand and placed it in hers and sat next to her on the bed. The room was completely silent besides the machines. Mark came into the ICU room. He had been visiting with the doctors. The doctors had told him that they should probably start to make arrangements to turn off the machines. I don't think he even realized I was there. I have tried many times to explain the expression of sadness that he had on his face, but I can never find the right words to describe it.

He said in a quiet, tender voice, "It is time, Lois. We need to start making arrangements."

Lois just stared at Kris, and then said back to Mark, "Let's make the arrangements."

Mark started to leave the room when Lois called him back in and told him to look at the heart monitor. The numbers started to drop until it reached a flat line. Kris died on her own in that instant. It was 10:25 a.m. It felt strange. It was like she was just hanging onto life and living until she knew she had the permission from her parents to go.

Her life was over. Her sixteen short years came to an end from a quiet, secret addiction that was so innocent. A beautiful girl who was trying to be something she felt like she wasn't.

I wanted her back; I needed her back. It had only been moments, but I already felt so completely lost and alone.

Where do I go from here? What am I supposed to do? No one had the answers. All the high school friends and classmates were still in the waiting area on the main floor. I knew that they would find out soon that she had died. I wasn't ready to face them. I don't remember leaving the room but I do remember walking toward the elevator.

Cammy, Kris's eleven-year-old sister, ran up to me and gave me a big hug. She said to me, "Deborah, just because Kris is gone doesn't mean you can't come over anymore." I just hugged her. Kris's stepmom was explaining to three-year-old Lindsey that Kris is in heaven now. She was using the My Little Pony to describe her going to heaven.

Doctors, nurses, friends, noises, and movement—all were going on around me, yet I felt quiet in my head, almost as if I were in my own world. I got on the elevator and went down through the waiting area. I was greeted by so many people. She had touched so many lives, and her death would do the same.

It is a weird feeling walking out of a hospital and leaving your friend. I felt like I was walking away from her. I needed to be close to her but away from everyone else.

I drove over to her house and went into her room. I crawled into her bed and just lay there, staring at everything. I could hear family downstairs and people talking. It was a weird comfort to me. I couldn't imagine being anywhere else.

I tried to understand exactly what happened to Kris.

―――――――――――――

Why did she die?

I'm not a doctor and can't fully explain it, but I can try.

The way I understand it, we all have hydrochloric acid in our stomachs to help us break down our food. If you take a teaspoon of baking soda, there will be a large amount of gas added to your stomach. In Kris's case, she may have taken up to half a box of baking soda. It caused so much gas, and it had nowhere to go. That is why she was so bloated and started to swell.

When she went into surgery, the doctors found out that she was having kidney failure. She also had liver damage and damage to her pancreas, and they had to take out parts of her intestine. She had a kink in her stomach, which closed off her esophagus. They didn't think her body could handle anymore. That is when they stopped and closed her up.

Kris had an eating disorder. She made a decision to take a large amount of baking soda that night to help her throw up. She died from that decision. An eating disorder caused that decision.

CHAPTER 2

friendship and purge

Before Kris died, no one I had ever known had ever died; death was not familiar to me. When she died, I felt as if a part of me died as well. Because her death was the result of an eating disorder, everyone thought I had one, too. My church leaders, schoolteachers, and classmates all assumed I had the same disorder. I had one teacher in particular that was on a mission to "fix" me. I explained to him that I was naturally thin and didn't have a problem—he didn't need to worry about me. But he wouldn't stop. It was so hard for me that I stopped attending his class.

Why was I left to fight Kris's battles? I felt like my life was about to become an open book since her journals would be read and what she did—we did—would be known. I didn't feel like that was fair. I felt nervous and scared.

I found myself pulling away from everyone and going through the motions just to get through the day. I felt like friends, family, classmates, and people that I didn't even know all of a sudden cared. Like they couldn't save Kris, so they thought they needed to save me.

I felt alone.

Kris and I had been together a lot—at church on Sundays and again on Tuesdays for youth group. We shared a locker at school, and she drove me to and from school every day since her sixteenth birthday. If we could be together, we were together; we shared each other's secrets and dreams for the future. We talked about going to college and then raising our kids together.

It seemed like I had known Kris my entire life, but, as it surprised some people, we only knew each other for four years.

Kris's dad invited her to go along with him on a business trip to Florida. He told her that she could invite a couple of friends to go with her, so she asked Marcy and Stephanie to go with her. Kris and I were friends, but we really didn't know each other very well. Marcy and Stephanie convinced her to let me come. I was so excited; it was a trip of a lifetime and we were given the royal treatment. We had never seen a hotel room that big. We danced and sang all around the room, having the time of our lives.

After dinner on our very first night, when we got back to our hotel room, she went right to the bathroom and threw up. It was the first time I witnessed her purging.

Marcy, Stephanie, and I were right outside the bathroom door and heard her throwing up. At first I thought she was sick, but she reassured me that she was fine. I remember Marcy looking at Stephanie and me, after hearing her and saying, "That was gross." It never crossed my mind that it was wrong. I just couldn't understand why you would want to do it.

We spent our days by the pool and shopping around the hotel. On one of our shopping days we went into a swimsuit shop. We all tried on many swimsuits, and Marcy, Stephanie, and I ended up buying the exact same one but in different colors. Kris bought a slightly different one because she thought the one we bought made her look fat. She didn't seem happy about herself and was critical of herself.

Kris and I were inseparable after that trip, and her mom would soon move to a house near my family, so we saw each other a lot more.

Kris had a lot of friends that really loved her and considered her a good friend. A few of those childhood friends recall what she was like growing up and before and after her parents' divorce. Rosemary and Michele were two of those friends, and the three of them were very close.

———————

ROSEMARY'S STORY

Kristin lived ninety-five years in her short sixteen years on this earth. Her life still has an impact on me. I learned a lot from her in the short decade we knew each other, and I still think of her often. Not only did she impact my life, but she has also impacted the lives of other young women who have heard and learned from her heartbreaking story.

I met Kristin when her family moved into our neighborhood when I was six. Although I was a year older, we became instant friends. I still know her phone number, and I would do anything to call it right now to hear her cheerful voice on the other end.

We were inseparable. If I wasn't at her house, she was at mine. My family was her family, and I felt at home with her parents and siblings. Her mom, Lois, would take us for rides in her red Mercedes-Benz. We would open the sunroof and blast the eight-track of Dolly Parton and the *three* of us would sing every word; Lois was one of the girls, too! Kristin and I had an incredible friendship. We often spent our Friday nights watching Johnny Carson at my house on a pull out couch. My cousin Michele, Kristin, and I shared laughter and tears during those sleepovers. I'll never forget the night she told us about her parents' divorce. She was upset and I was grateful for the friendship we shared and that I could be there for her during those hard times.

At her dad's house we memorized every step of Michael Jackson's *Thriller* video and perfected the moonwalk. Our summers were filled with riding our bikes or taking the bus from our house to the mall to eat lunch. We enjoyed hot, lazy summer days sunbathing at my pool lathered in baby oil on overinflated inner tubes. I loved riding her dad's horses down to the local creek. I will never forget the summer of 1983 when we sandbagged that same creek to protect her dad's home and our neighborhood from the wall of water rushing down the creek bed.

Kristin and I spent time at my parents' cabin and enjoyed every season in the outdoors. My favorite memories were those of us just talking on the phone.

She loved children, and we would babysit together for many neighbors. It wasn't uncommon for us to buy the same clothes without knowing. We knew each other inside and out.

Kristin even arranged for my first kiss on my sixteenth birthday. Her dad was friends with a member of The Commodores and was able to get us front row seats and backstage passes to the Lionel Richie concert. We were able to meet Lionel Richie backstage, and he gave me a sweet sixteen kiss on the cheek after the concert.

Kristin's joyful energy was contagious, and I wanted to be with her every waking moment. She loved life. She was a magnet of positive energy and fun! Everyone wanted to be friends with Kristin. Not just for her beautiful exterior, but for her joyful personality. She impacted me for good. Her positive attitude is something that I still strive to maintain in my own life. She taught me how to laugh, cry, and love unconditionally. She taught me the meaning of how to love family and friends. Even though she had her share of struggles, she never showed it to me on the outside. I wish I had known the pain she was experiencing inside.

Although we stayed close, we didn't spend as much time together after junior high. Her parents divorced and her mother moved. They didn't move far, but it was painful for me not having her around the corner anymore. Our circles of friends changed, and I didn't realize the extent of the secret she was keeping.

I was at a party once when Kristin and a group of girls were making themselves throw up. I didn't participate, and I didn't think it was anything other than some teenage experimentation. Eating disorders weren't something that people were very aware of. Karen Carpenter had died three years earlier from anorexia. I knew of bulimia and I knew Kristin had made herself throw up, but I didn't really realize that her behavior was an eating disorder.

On May 1, 1986, I was in a hurry to leave school. Kristin was standing at her locker. She always looked beautiful. Kristin was always sporting the most stylish clothes, beautiful natural blonde curls, and gorgeous face with a perfect nose and sparkling, smiling blue eyes. That day she was wearing Guess brand denim overalls with embroidered planes on the front pocket and a red T-shirt. I stopped to visit with her and she said she would call me that evening. I went home and didn't hear from her. I didn't think much of it and knew we could talk the next day at school.

The next day changed my life forever. Images of Kristin standing by her locker flooded my mind. That image is still vivid in my memory. I wish I had known then that at that moment I would never see her again in this life. I think of everything I would have done differently. I would have hugged her. I would have told her how much I love her. But I am so grateful that I have that last image of her smiling.

I'm so grateful that we had those ten years together. My mom always said, "You both were angel friends in heaven, because I've never seen you argue. You always keep each other happy." Now that angel friend watches over all of us here on earth.

After Kristin's death I went into a state of depression. I couldn't sleep, I couldn't eat, and I didn't want to move on. A few days after her death, her dad called me up and asked me to come to his house. He was preparing photos for the funeral and wanted me to help. He had hundreds of photos laid out on his kitchen countertops. It was fun to relive the memories through those photographs. We both laughed and cried knowing that all we had were the memories. No Kristin, no more fun times with my best friend, no more sparkling blue eyes.

She had a beautiful funeral, but I wanted someone to wake me up and tell me it was all a horrible nightmare. The weeks after were some of my darkest. Everyone continued on with his or her life and I wanted everyone to stop. My world stopped when she died and I didn't want anyone to forget her. I was worried her bright light would eventually fade away.

I would go to her graveside and sit and talk to her for hours. I was angry with her; I was angry at what she thought she had to be. I knew deep down that Kristin would want me to be happy. My faith helped me realize that she was in a better place. But the situation didn't make me feel better.

I went to a girl's camp that summer and visited with someone there who was new to our group. I shared Kristin's story and she shared with me that she was struggling with similar problems. I encouraged her to get the help she needed. It scared me to think that someone could be bulimic like Kristin—that someone's eating disorder could change the course of his or her life and the lives of those that love him or her. My anger about bulimia turned into a question: how could I help someone get assistance with his or her problem?

During my college years I shared my story with my sorority sisters, and some even told me that they remembered reading about Kristin in the newspaper. I know that Kristin's story has saved many girls.

I am now a middle-aged woman and have had opportunity to tell Kristin's story to youth groups in my church organization. The pain is still very real to me. I keep in touch with her family. This experience made us all family. I know that Kristin still lives on. I feel her presence; I know that I will see her again. I know that it will be a joyous reunion.

MICHELE'S STORY

It's hard to believe that it's been twenty-eight years since Kris died. It used to be that not a day went by when I didn't think about her or something would remind me of her. I still think about her and, every once in a while, I dream about her. There are a few different scenarios that play out in my head: either it was a mistake and she never died, or she moved away and we finally got back in touch with each other. Either way, when I wake up and realize that neither is true, I am left with a sad feeling.

Kristin was my best friend in elementary and middle school. She, my cousin Rosemary, and I were always together. She was always the leader, and we would have such a great time. One summer we decided to have a kids' camp or school where the neighbor kids would come to Kristin's house and we would do fun activities with them. I'm pretty sure she came up with the idea. She would have been a great mother or teacher or anything for that matter. We slept over at each other's houses all the time. If my mom couldn't find me, she could always bet I was at Kristin's house. I basically had two families. I was pretty lucky to have a friend like her.

Because of Kristin, I did things I never thought I'd do. I took ballet, other dance lessons, and singing lessons, learned how to snow ski, and so much more. If you asked me who I wanted to be when I grew up, I would have said Kristin.

I don't know when it started but somewhere in the last few years of Kristin's life, she felt that she wasn't skinny enough and wanted to feel better about herself. I felt the same way. We loved to eat but didn't love what it did to our bodies. We took aerobics classes to help, but it didn't seem like it was doing anything. Then she told me she'd found out a new way to lose weight. All you had to do was make yourself throw up by sticking your finger down your throat.

It sounded simple enough; what would it hurt? I, however, couldn't ever do it. I tried, but it didn't work. I envied Kristin because she could do it. I couldn't ever tell if she lost weight or not.

One night after dinner with my family, I decided to go try it again. I went into the bathroom and started gagging, but my mom heard me and immediately came in asking what I was doing. She got mad at me and said that was not a good thing to do. I was so embarrassed that my mom had found out that I never did it again. The sad thing is that if I could have made myself do it, I would have, and I don't think my mom getting mad would have stopped me. I seriously didn't think it was that bad.

No one had ever heard of bulimia at that time, and never in my wildest dreams would I have thought it would have such a horrible outcome. During this time, Kristin was moving to another neighborhood, and we didn't hang out as much together any more. I thought she was done with the "throwing up" thing. She never talked about it anymore.

She meant so much to me. She was such a huge part of my life. Even if we didn't see as much of each other during that last year before she died, we were still friends. After all, she helped me become who I am today.

After Kristin's death, life continued on, but there was a big hole in my heart; I tried to carry on as usual, but everything reminded me of her. Even a year later, I still had a hard time moving on. I got through it by looking to God for answers. My religion teaches that we will see our loved ones again someday, so I took solace in the fact that, even though it would be hard, I would be able to see her again and that she was in a better place.

Twenty-eight years later, I still hold on to those beliefs, and I still think of her; I am stronger now because I know that her story can help others. If it only helped one person to break away from the hold that bulimia has on him or her, then her passing was not in vain. I want her memory to live on. By giving my daughter Kristin's name (Janessa Kristin Cunningham), I wanted Janessa to know what a wonderful person Kristin was and how she was a leader and was liked by everyone. I wanted to instill those qualities in my daughter and to let her know that even though Kristin's life was cut short, it could be a lesson to her and other girls that you can overcome hard things by sharing your problems with someone. I wanted to teach my daughter not to keep secrets, even if they may seem small.

I wish Kristin would have had the chance to overcome bulimia, but back then not much was known about it, and even after she was told it wasn't good to continue doing it, I know that she didn't think her life would be taken from her because of what she was doing to herself. In her mind she was trying to better herself. But now, because of her story and others like it, something can be done. Now people are more aware it. I guess that was the good that came from her death.

STEPHANIE'S STORY

When I was halfway through the second grade, my family moved and I started at a new elementary school. My new teacher was Ms. Reeves. She introduced me to the class that first day and asked a darling, quiet, studious little girl named Marcy to show the new girl—me—around the school; however, before Marcy could respond, a vivacious little girl across the room shouted from her seat, "No, no, I will Ms. Reeves; I will show her around."

Her name was Kristin, and from that time forward, she and I became fast friends, with Marcy quietly leading us in the right direction, always the voice of reason. The three of us did many things together, but when Kristin and I were on our own, there was no telling what would happen.

Kristin was the adventurous one who was never afraid to take a risk; for some reason I was always quick to follow her. She was the first to introduce me to the possibility of eating dry cake mix directly out of the box with a spoon. She made me a radish sandwich with white bread, mayonnaise, and mustard, with the radishes sliced and perfectly placed upon the bread. I thought she was so grown up to make a sandwich like that. I still eat them today.

We made lemonade stands, and once I ran and hid behind a bush when a cute boy came to get a drink. Meanwhile, Kristin, ever the assertive salesperson, ended up selling him three cups.

My favorite place to go was a place she introduced to me. Kristen, Marcy, and I called it our secret garden. Our secret garden was a small grove of trees with a little brook running through it. We would take our dolls there and have tea parties. We would sing and play and stay there for hours. We all loved each other very much.

The three of us began doing many activities together. Marcy joined us in taking classes at a dance studio. Kristin and I took a sewing class, art classes, and a dollhouse furniture–making class.

As tenderhearted as Kristin was, she had a feisty way about her. For instance, one day in the third grade I came back to school after being sick. I was looking around for my chair, and I found Kristin sitting in it. I stood beside her and asked her to please return my chair. She said nothing and stared at the chalkboard as if I weren't there. I went to the other side of the chair and asked her once again, "May I please have my chair?" Still not a word from her. I stood in front of her and put my face in hers and asked, "Kristin, can I please have my chair back?"

She looked at me with squinty eyes, said, "No," and then slapped me right across the cheek.

I told the teacher, hoping to get some sympathy and to get her on my side. Somehow we both ended up having to stay in for recess. We decided that we would apologize since it was easier than being enemies. We started laughing; in fact, we laughed so hard during our punishment that we wet our pants. The teacher sent us outside to dry. We thought it was a great way to get a break from the mundane daily routine. The teacher didn't think it was quite so funny.

Now that I think about it, I never did get my chair back.

As time went on, the freedoms of childhood gave way to the realities of adulthood. Kristin's life changed as she dealt with the challenge of her parents' divorce. Divorce in those days was not readily accepted. I also came from a broken home, so I knew all too well the challenges she faced.

Kristin had to learn how to appreciate a new stepmom while feeling the need to protect her own mother. Her time was split between her mother's home and her father's home. Each home had very different rules. To cope with this, Kristin made up her own rules.

We were coming into our "between" years during this time. We were discovering boys and seeking the freedoms we expected we should have. Both of us developed somewhat of an attitude. Kristin pulled it off better than I did. She could light up the room with her twinkling eyes and sunshiny disposition. She was a candle in a dark room. She always tried to make everyone feel comfortable and, more importantly, loved.

By the time we got to the seventh grade, we added a fourth friend—Deborah—to the group. She was a blast and always made us laugh. The four of us were always very busy in athletics or dance. This kept us all quite slim and trim and yet, in our dance studio, very thin, very muscular dancers surrounded us.

Marcy had the ballerina body and the talent. Our new friend, Deborah, was tall and thin and could eat whatever she wanted (Funyons, Coke, and French fries every day) without gaining a pound. Kris and I sometimes felt like we were just along for the ride. Neither of us had much talent. At least Kristin was petite and had all the right curves. I felt like my thighs were much too big and probably more appropriate for a linebacker.

In the dance studio, girls who were very thin, with almost gaunt-looking faces, surrounded us. Binging and purging became a topic of discussion among the girls. Looking back now, I wonder if Kristin started to feel pressure that she was supposed to look like them. I thought she was darling; all the boys liked her. However, I think when she looked in the mirror she saw something different than what I saw. She had twinkly eyes; beautiful, blonde curly hair; and a smile that sparkled—somehow she stopped seeing that.

As we moved toward our teen years, all four of us were making changes, some of which our parents didn't appreciate. At times we found ourselves at odds with them and with each other. The reasons why fail my memory now, but through the lens of time I am sure they were of little consequence.

We were starting junior high school, and suddenly the pressures started to become more intense. It was just the silly things that were very real to teenagers—things like wearing the "right" clothes, being friends with the "right" people, and having the "right" look.

We were still close, but junior high introduced us (me) to a lot more people. I began spending more and more time with other friends. When Kristin moved to live with her mom, it made getting to her house harder, and we ended up spending less and less time together, but I still saw her when I could.

When we were sophomores in high school, we felt like a whole new world was opening up to us. We were making new friends, both male and female, and our hobbies started to change. There was more pressure now than there had been in junior high to look a certain way or act a certain way to try to be popular. Some of these pressures came between Kristin and me. We still considered ourselves as friends, but the distance between us began to grow. Kristin was spending more time with Deborah while I was seeing other friends. Nevertheless, when we got together, we still felt very close.

I have a stack of letters from her—many of them begging to know if we were still friends. We were, but we just had different things going on in our lives that separated us from time to time. Later, as I reviewed Kristin's letters, I started to recognize the insecurities she suffered. And I questioned why.

This was the girl whose life I wanted to live. She was so cute, so bubbly, and so hilarious. So many people loved her, and she reciprocated that love and kindness to everyone. She was a good student and talented in so many ways. She had an amazing, brilliant mother and a successful father.

My thought is that Kristin was missing something inside and sometimes tried to fill that void with the wrong things. Her parents' divorce impacted her, and it just seemed like she was often looking for outside affirmations.

In a few of her letters, she stated, "life was so boring" and "I want something exciting to happen so badly." It was odd because her life was anything but boring. She often traveled with her dad. She had gone with him to Egypt and other exotic places. He did other fun things with her like taking her to see and meet Lionel Richie. She was always doing things that were fun and exciting. Somehow, though, it just didn't seem to be enough. She still felt there was a hole, and she was always futilely trying to fill it.

Apparently, Kristin had been binging and purging for quite some time—probably six months or longer. As I realized this, I became really worried about her. I confronted her about it. She was embarrassed but assured me that it was no big deal. I disagreed with her, but she became defensive and ignored my opinions.

Out of great concern, hurt, and fear, I shared this information with her father and later with her mother, Lois. I felt relieved knowing that I had done what I could, and I felt confident that they would take care of it. Once home, life went on as normal.

I was concerned for Kristin, but when I saw that she looked and seemed fine, I didn't think she was really doing any damage. Kristin could eat whatever she wanted (and as *much* as she wanted). Then all she had to do was throw it up and she wouldn't gain any weight, as far as I could tell. I decided that this really was a way one could have one's cake and eat it, too, so I started binging and purging for a short time. I didn't continue, however, because I didn't like doing it, nor did I like the way I felt.

That's when I had my "ah-ha" moment. I asked myself, *Why don't I just eat right and exercise?* From that moment on, I tried to eat healthier, and I became more active in dance and track. I just felt better with this sort of lifestyle, and the habits I developed then have stuck with me ever since. I continue to be active with cycling, and I became much more nutritionally conscientious.

Right before Kristin died, Madonna released a new song called "Live to Tell." Kristin told to me that it was her favorite song. As I listened to that song, I realized that it foreshadowed what was shortly to occur. After her death, each time it would come on the radio, I would cry, and cry out loud, "But you didn't; you didn't live to tell your secrets or the pain you were hiding."

It has been almost thirty years since Kristin's passing. The impact it has left on my life has been profound. Her sudden death took some time grieving and adjusting. Kristin and I went to the same church and it was the God that we both believed that I asked why He would allow her to go. It was a very dark time in my life. For refuge I would often write her letters and take them to her grave. I wrote her of my anger toward her for abusing her body, for not recognizing her beauty, and for leaving me.

There was always a peaceful feeling at her grave, and I drew comfort from the thought of her presence. I believe in angels on earth, the people that are placed in our paths, and I also believe in angels in heaven that guide us through life's journey. I have felt she has been like an angel watching over me. I have felt her in my thoughts; my dreams and her gentle nudges have led me in the right direction.

Kristin's story became well known throughout the central Utah area. I was astonished to hear that my cousin's teacher was using Kristin's story as a study in a class called American Problems. I did not realize until then that bulimia was becoming an epidemic. I, too, have used Kristin's story many times to help peers that were struggling with body image and eating disorders.

As I got older, it was teens that I shared her story with in hopes that they would recognize that their bodies are a gift from a loving God. I wanted them to know that a perfect God made each one of us for a purpose and "God doesn't make junk." I have shared how her life and death affected not only me but also everyone around her.

I realized that we think that because these are our bodies, we can do what we want with them. The danger in this mindset is that it doesn't affect your body alone; it affects everybody that knows you and loves you. This advice, as well as Kristin's story, may have had a role in saving the lives of young women whom I met while teaching an aerobic class in New York City.

I chose a life of health and fitness in large part because of Kristin's struggles. I did not want the same struggles in my life. A young woman came to New York to be admitted into a hospital program for girls with eating disorders. She was encouraged by what I could tell her of the love that people had towards Kristin and saw how it had pierced my own heart. She began to see things from a different perspective and felt that she, too, might be loved the same way. The program was successful, and she triumphed through her disorder beautifully.

I am still not completely sure why Kris had to die, but I do know that her story has been beneficial to many. Every September, I am reminded that Kristin and I would be turning another year older together, and I often wondered if we would have had similar lives. The pain in my heart continues, and I still find myself crying occasionally for her loss.

However, knowing what I know now, I have found that I may be parenting with a different lens than I would have otherwise. I teach my children to eat healthy and live an active lifestyle. I try very hard not to focus on weight, but instead to focus on happy and healthy living. I continue in my career as a personal trainer and a Pilates instructor. I often remind my clients how beautiful they are, to stand tall, and to love the bodies they have been given.

Kristin's legacy will continue on throughout out generations—her light that shined so bright and the light that went out with her death.

MARCY'S STORY

I can't remember a time when Kristin wasn't there. When did she move into my neighborhood? First grade? Kindergarten? We were really little—roaming our homes, yards, and neighborhood and swimming in her pool. I spent so much time at her house, my parents used to call me Marcy Haroldsen. She had a bunk bed that I thought was so cool and a "pit" to watch TV in and a big wooded yard.

Her dad had a girlfriend. Once we snuck into the living room when he was entertaining, and she pulled the girlfriend's picture out of a guitar case to show me. Then we were chased out of the room.

She showed me how to melt cheese in the microwave for a snack. She was a blast—funny, joking, laughing, kidding, and always ready to smile and giggle. She was adventurous and kind of mischievous, but everybody loved her.

I often couldn't get away to her house without my little sister Kia tagging along because Kia loved Kristin, too. To make matters worse, Kristin seemed to like Kia more than me. But Kristin loved everyone and wanted to have fun with whoever was willing.

I loved it when we would go to their family condo in the mountains and sleep in the bed that pulled out of the wall. I also loved it when we went ice skating. We had the rink all to ourselves and would skate for hours, learning how to go backwards, do figure eights, and go in circles. That was the best. In the summer, she would come to our cabin by the lake, where we would water ski and kneeboard and ride the "death sled."

I believe we were in the sixth grade when her parents got a divorce. I remember Kristin being unspeakably sad about that and not liking the switching from house to house that ensued. Nothing seemed right after the divorce. It was better when we were small and played in the first house. Having to visit two strange houses later was awkward.

Kristin seemed to become more angry and defiant with the divorce. She was still fun, but with an edge. Most of the anger was directed at her dad. So maybe that was why he let her bring Deborah, Stephanie, and me to Florida. He was the best chaperone ever—not there except for dinnertime.

We heard her throw up one night after dinner, but honestly, I don't remember her throwing up again until our sophomore year. Why didn't I realize this was something really bad? Why didn't I say more to her than, "Eeeew, gross!" while we were in Florida? Would anything I could have done or said have made any difference?

I wish Kristin were here today. I wish she could have grown up with all of us, fallen in and out of love a dozen times, found someone worthy of her, and had a marriage full of all the ups and downs and great things marriage has to offer—especially children. I want to know her now, her husband, and her children. I want her to come on our weekends and lunches with the friends.

I miss Kristin. I'm still mad, and it's a tragedy that she died when she was only just beginning. If only she didn't make herself throw up. If only she knew she was fun and beautiful and so awesome and didn't need to throw up or change to be better. I wish she knew she was good enough just as she was. I don't know if I will be mad or happy when I see Kristin again. I will want to be mad, but she will smile, and then laugh, and I won't be mad anymore.

Just a couple days after Kristin died, I was crying angrily on my way out the door to hang out with Deb and Steph (the only ones who knew and understood exactly how I felt) when my mom said, "You are going to have to stop acting like this soon, Marcy. Life goes on." Hearing that only made me more upset.

I desperately didn't want life to go on without Kristin. That would mean forgetting her, growing up and apart from how we had been at sixteen, fifteen, fourteen, thirteen . . . all the way back to how we had been as small children. The pain of losing Kristin was so unbearable at first and still brings tears to my eyes, but I have learned to live with that hole in my heart. I know I will see Kristin again and that I will be able to renew our cherished friendship—thanks to parents and teachers who taught me from a very young age of hope and love and truth.

Now I am a wife and stay-at-home mother of six children: one boy and five girls, ages ranging from five to sixteen. They all know the story of Kristin's death, and we discuss body image and healthy eating habits a lot. My children are all shapes and sizes, and I tell them they must be happy with the body God gave them. Everybody is different, so don't compare. And never criticize or judge someone else. Eat right and exercise, then get on with the rest of your life. That's what every mom should tell her children.

I have another dear friend who maybe didn't hear these truths as a child, and I wish I could help her believe them.

She is nineteen years old and has been suffering for about four years from anorexia. I watched her physical transformation and still weep at how powerless I am in begging her to stop.

Stop.

Just stop before her family and friends lose her, too.

When she first went into the Center for Change, I called her mother in a panic and told her briefly about Kristin, telling her that her daughter could die and that this is very, very serious. How foolish of me. I'm quite sure her mother already knew that. I've written my friend during her subsequent visits to hospitals and centers, and so have many others. As she continues to struggle with this disease, I want her to know I love her anyway and she is beautiful.

That's what I would tell Kristin if I could go back to being sixteen again.

You are beautiful.

You are crazy fun to be around.

You are unbelievably important to many, many people.

You don't need to throw up your meals.

We all love you just the way you are.

If you want to be thinner, I will go jogging with you and let's eat salad for lunch instead of Frostys and french fries. Look in the mirror and see a life worth living, because your life is priceless to us and we don't want to live without you.

I am so glad that Kris had so many good friends. As you can see, she was easy to be around. I think we all wish that we would have just spoken up. If you know of someone that has an eating disorder, tell someone. Get them help even if it means they might get mad at you. It is a chance worth taking, trust me. If you truly love them, you will get them help. If you are the one suffering, you may think that having an eating disorder only affects you and it's not hurting anyone else. That's not the case; you are hurting everyone around you that loves you.

Florida was the first time I heard Kris purge. It became something that she started to do a lot when we were together. I became used to her doing it. Kris was a fun, bubbly, outgoing girl, as you have heard from several friends. We always had fun together, and sometimes our ideas were a little crazy.

One night we decided to go to her family's condo in the mountains, but we knew that our parents were going to say no. So she told her dad that she was spending the night at my home, and I told my dad the same thing. We got Marcy and Stephanie to come with us. Kris picked me up in the big family van. We were hyper and excited. We went to dinner and stuffed ourselves before we drove up. We had the music cranked up in the car, and we were singing as loud as we could. We were happy and life was good.

We got to the condo, and we all thought we were so smart. We turned on the music in the condo and we were dancing around. Then the condo phone rang; we had to have only been there less than an hour. I answered it and it was my dad. He said that Kris's father figured out where we were and he was sending the police over. He told us to leave and come home right away. We were bummed, but it didn't spoil our mood. We thought that we were so clever and decided to write on a paper plate, "Dear officer, we've been bad, we've been here, and now we're gone." We stuck it on the condo door. As we piled in the van to head home, Kris had an idea. I feel like she felt we were invincible and had a fabulous idea that wasn't so fabulous. She climbed up through the van sunroof onto the top of the van; we had to be going at least eighty miles an hour coming down the canyon. I was driving and Stephanie was taking photos of Kris's face squished against the windshield. We were taking our time getting home because we knew we were going to be in a lot of trouble.

By the time I was dropped off, my dad was sitting in the front room waiting for me, wanting to talk and explain my punishment. He wasn't very happy with me but told me he was glad I was home and safe. Even though we did dumb stuff, I never thought something could happen to us. We were going to live forever, and we had our entire lives ahead of us. By the time I had met Kris, her parents were already divorced and her mom moved by us. That's when Kris left a lot of those childhood friends and we started to hang out. She would continue to be friends with them, but they wouldn't carry the burden of knowing her secret to the end— that she was still making herself throw up. I think that many of them thought she had stopped or was doing it only a few times.

I have said this before. I didn't know throwing up after eating was necessarily wrong, and I didn't know it had a name. I was the friend who would wonder "if only" forever. If only I had really spoken up—spoken up to her to stop, spoken up to her parents. But, as I reflect back, I really don't think I would have done anything different because I didn't know it was wrong. I know that none of us thought that it could or would ultimately kill her.

Kris was a beautiful girl who had her entire life ahead of her. She felt like she didn't fit into the stereotype of what the world seems to think you need to look like, and because of that, she was bulimic.

Almost three decades have gone by since Kris died, yet bulimia is still as much a problem today as it was then. The only difference is that people know the name now and they know it is an eating disorder. We must help stop girls from falling into this problem of feeling like they have to look like the girls in the magazines. We must educate them on how to be healthy and eat right.

We *must* speak up.

CHAPTER 3

parents' perspective

WRITTEN BY MARK O. HAROLDSEN, FATHER OF KRISTIN HAROLDSEN

On April 30, 1986, I received a phone call that shocked and saddened me to my very core, but the events of the next two days were much, much worse and by far the worst of my entire life. I had just left my former wife, Lois's house after having a wonderful visit with my kids and Lois when my cell phone rang. Lois gave me the terrible and tragic news that our good friends David and Linda Cowan's teenage son, Davy—a great kid and a good friend of my teenage kids—had just died.

I flipped a U-turn on busy Highland Drive and raced back to Lois's house and went straight to my sixteen-year-old daughter and gave her a massive hug, telling her how much I loved her. My instinct told me she was at a critical and vulnerable stage of her life and that she was dealing with some big issues. I was worried about her.

About one year before that night, I had taken Kristin halfway around the world to surprise my mother on Mother's Day. My parents had lived in Cairo, Egypt, for six months, and I took Kristin there because I wanted to spend time with her. I could feel and see that she had some big struggles and challenges that she was dealing with that were different from what her siblings were dealing with.

We had a great trip, and I felt that we had bonded better than any time before. On that trip, Kristin shared many of her inner thoughts, emotions, and struggles. But on that April 30, I didn't feel as confident about that bond and was beginning to realize that Kristin had not opened up as much as I thought she had in Egypt. Sadly, I soon found out that my drop in confidence was correct.

Two days later, my sweet, wonderful, full-of-fun-and-life Kristin was dead. Believe me when I say there are no words in the English language to describe the horrendous and devastating feeling that parents have when their child dies. Unless someone has experienced this terrible, life-jolting event, I don't think any person can understand the hell parents go through. And I hope beyond hope that you *never* have to experience losing your child and that maybe what I am writing and this book can save others that are facing and dealing with any form of an eating disorder. Children are not supposed to die before their parents.

After dinner on May 1, I got another call from Lois telling me she was at Cottonwood Hospital with Kristin. Right after dinner, Kristin had taken some baking soda to make herself throw up. Lois told me that I really didn't need to come to the hospital because Kristin was about to have her stomach pumped and would be going home soon after.

Disregarding Lois's comment, I jumped in my car and sped to the hospital. As soon as I arrived I was told that they were unsuccessful with the attempt to pump Kristin's stomach. Her esophagus had twisted, making it impossible to get the tube to the stomach.

Being a proactive guy who is usually in control (or at least I think I am), I was beyond upset as I felt totally and utterly lacking of any control whatsoever. An hour or two later (I really can't remember how long it was), they wheeled Kristin's bed toward the operating room. The nurses told Lois and me that cutting Kristin open was the only way to relieve the huge pressure, as her stomach was extremely bloated and as hard as a rock.

I found out later that her distended stomach was cutting off the blood supply to her vital organs, which can only survive without blood for about thirty minutes. Unfortunately, the internist doctor was on call, and it seemed like it took forever for him to get to the hospital to perform the necessary surgery.

The last words that Kristin and I spoke to each other were words of love. I told her how much I loved her, and she kept telling me how much she loved me and that she was so sorry for what she had done. To that comment I replied that it was OK and everything was going to be all right, but inside my head I was not as confident as my words.

Dear, sweet Kristin never regained consciousness after surgery. She had multiple organ failures due to lack of blood flow. The next morning the doctor approached Lois and me to tell us that although Kristin was still alive, she had no brain activity and most of her internal organs had died. He then asked for permission to turn off her life support systems.

I can't begin to tell you how scrambled and wiped out my brain was at this point. All of this happened in less than sixteen hours. Just sixteen hours before, Kristin was full of life and energy—she was perfectly healthy. Those sixteen hours had fried my brain and now the doctor was asking if I agreed to turn off some machines and let my daughter die. I wanted to scream at him! I wanted to know what took him so damn long to get to the hospital. I wanted my Kristin back. I wanted my life to be like it was a few days before.

Lois and I talked and finally concluded that we didn't have much choice. But we asked the doctor to wait until we had talked to our kids who were waiting outside the intensive care unit along with what seemed like half of the kids from Cottonwood High School.

As I walked toward the door, I could hear the steady rhythmic beating of Kristin's heart monitor. Halfway to the door the beeping began to slow. As I reached the door, suddenly the beeping stopped, and the flat line sound loudly screamed into my ears. Kristin was gone. She had not been unhooked from the machines, but it was as if she was watching us and didn't want her parents to worry or even think about the decision to turn off the machines.

Days later at the funeral, a lady came up to me and said, "I lost a child, and I am here to tell you, you *never* get over it." I didn't need to hear that; it absolutely crushed me. I wanted to slap her or scream at her, but years later (it's now been twenty-seven years) I understand what she meant, and she was right. However, I now would say even though you never get over it, you can and do learn how to live with it, and even learn some life-changing lessons.

Looking back, I missed so many signals that I should have picked up on as far as recognizing the behaviors of someone with an eating disorder. (I had never even heard of bulimia.) Early on I found out that Kristin was making herself throw up, but I certainly didn't think this was life threatening. Nevertheless, both Lois and I were very concerned, and we talked to Kristin about it.

I later found out that she thought she looked fat, which was not even close to being true; she was slender and beautiful. I learned—much later—that most people with bulimia or anorexia really believe they are fat, but most are not; they just see themselves that way.

Long before Kristin's death she told us that she had stopped the bulimia thing, which I wanted to believe, and did. Again, I should have picked up on her frequent trips to the bathroom after meals, and, knowing what I know now, I would have listened through the door and taken stronger actions to get professional help. If you are a parent and have any suspicions, I strongly recommend you closely monitor and get help for your loved one.

After Kirstin's surgery the night of May 1, I was so full of fear and rage. I was furious at the doctor for not being at the hospital and so very, very mad at myself for not being in control and being unable to help my Kristin. I was mad at myself for not recognizing what was really going on.

With all this anger and fury I did something really stupid and hurtful. I left the hospital and drove directly to the house of Kristin's best friend, Deborah Pedersen's. She greeted me at the door, and I verbally attacked this sweet, wonderful sixteen-year-old, accusing her of hiding the truth from me that Kristin was still purging herself after most meals.

To this day I regret trying to blame someone who was totally innocent. Looking back, my only excuse could be that my brain was so scrambled—I was a total mess. Deborah, I am so sorry; please forgive me.

Now, all these years later, I hope with all my heart and soul that the words I am putting on this paper will help others, both parents and friends and anyone that is struggling with an eating disorder. This terrible addiction *can* be cured and lives can be saved if action is taken.

For the first year at least after Kristin died, I totally withdrew from my friends, my business, and, to a degree, my family. I was so devastated that I couldn't, or wouldn't, or at least did not want to deal with anything. I just thought life at that point was totally worthless, and I sat around feeling sorry for myself. And, yes, I did a ton of crying! That first year after Kristin died, I died with her and did a bit of drinking—which seemed to help, or at least it dulled my mind to the point it didn't hurt quite so much.

I remember well that about a year later I finally agreed to give a speech in St. Louis. After my speech, I recall going to my hotel room and having a gigantic melt down, coming totally apart, and now, even as I write this, it's getting to me again. But that night in my hotel room was the beginning of a huge positive and life-changing turnaround.

As I recovered from my massive meltdown in that hotel room that night, I remembered back when my seventeen-year-old brother, Bruce, died right in front of me on the basketball court in Ankara, Turkey, when I was a mere fifteen years old. I saw my parents react in horror as I told them that night what had happened. Then I saw them in total depression for a very long time, pulling back from me and my brother and sister. That pullback hurt us even more, and as I sat in my hotel room in St. Louis that night, I decided that I just had to step up, quit feeling sorry for myself, and be a full-time, nonmourning father to my kids. I'm pretty sure that saved me as well as my children.

I have told Kristin's story—the good and the bad—many, many, many times, and even wrote about her and what happened, thinking that her story may help others.

It took a long time, but I finally did see something positive that came from the tragic death of Kristin. It has helped me to be more human. I am so much more empathetic and compassionate that I ever dreamed possible. I have realized that there are so many people—millions—who have had more tragedy in their lives. I think of the families in Syria or Egypt or Africa that have lost children and brothers, sisters, mothers, and fathers, sometimes in a matter of minutes or days.

I think of how it has been for Lois, Mark E,. David, Nicky, Cammy, Marcus, George, and Lindsey. How Kristin has touched all of our lives. I certainly wish she was still with us, but I am grateful for the light she was for us while we had her.

―――――――

WRITTEN BY LOIS HAROLDSEN, MOTHER OF KRISTIN HAROLDSEN

It was the spring of 1986. Nearly a year before (in the summer of 1985) I had bought a new house and moved in with my five children: Mark E., Kristin, Nicky, David, and Cammy. It was a lovely two-story home on a wooded lot on a quiet street in Salt Lake City, Utah. The house was only a couple of miles away from the home where the children had spent most of their young lives, so they were not changing schools or friends. Mark was a senior and Kristin was a sophomore at Cottonwood High School. David was in the eighth grade at Bonneville Junior High and my youngest two girls, Nicky and Cammy, were in fifth and sixth grade at Oakwood Elementary.

Everyone seemed to be happy with the new house and was adjusting to the new neighborhood. Life appeared to be happy. Of course, normal frustrations were the order of the day; teenage problems and sibling rivalry that seem to be every family's lot were part of our life as well.

I had been asked to direct a roadshow (a miniature production) for our church. Roadshows are fifteen-minute skits with lots of music and no plot written by someone who doesn't know how to write and directed by someone who doesn't know how to direct. Add to that performers who cannot act and will not come to rehearsals, and one might ask why we do them. We do them because we have been participating in road-shows forever and because they give everyone in our church a chance to perform on stage and have fun together.

I agreed to direct this one because I was the new kid on the block, and I thought it would be a good way to get to know people. I knew that all my children could participate and that it would help them to meet the kids in our new ward. I also suspected that, considering the ages of my children, it would probably be the last project I could get the whole bunch of us to participate in together.

Our life was busy, if not hectic. Each of the children was involved with friends and school, and I had the roadshow to worry about in addition to my regular routine of volunteer jobs and friends.

I had been single for five years since my divorce from the children's father, Mark. Because Mark is a successful and well-known businessman, our divorce had a certain amount of notoriety; yet it had been accomplished with little bitterness, and we worked well together as parents. Mark had remarried, and I was dating some, but we still made decisions together concerning our children's welfare. Their time was divided between houses (a feat we could accomplish because we lived so close to each other), but the children attended church with me each week.

A divorce is always traumatic in children's lives, and I was to find later that each of my children was affected in a different way. Mark had chosen a different path than I did in relation to our church, which was confusing to them in some ways. But we both love our children deeply and want the best for them. I have come to believe that, even in the most difficult circumstances, children can learn truth and then find their own ways to its fulfillment. Perhaps ours was not a traditional family lifestyle, but it was busy and happy, and it was ours.

One morning during that period of time, the woman who was helping me clean my house, Shirley, was upstairs in Kristin's bathroom. Our house had a guest bedroom and Kristin had quickly claimed it when we first went through the house. Shirley not only helped to keep our family in order but she was also a friend, and she came to me, worried.

"I don't know if it's my business," she said, "but I've found splashes on Krissy's toilet seat, and I think she's throwing up." I was shocked and horrified. As we talked, Shirley told me about a friend of hers who was bulimic in high school. Fifteen years later, her friend had to go to the doctor every day for vitamin shots because her body could no longer assimilate nutrients from food. She had miscarriage after miscarriage because she could not maintain a pregnancy. The consequences of this behavior were more frightening that I'd ever imagined.

The minute Kristin got home from school, I said to her, "I know that you are making yourself throw up to maintain your weight. It's really dangerous, and you have to quit!"

I told her about Shirley's friend, knowing that if I reasoned with this bright young woman, she would see my point and stop. In fact, her response assured me that this was true.

"I know it's dumb, Mom," she said. "I know it's dangerous, and I don't do it very much. I won't do it again."

I believed Kristin, and I still think that she intended to keep her promise. But I was not blind to the distress that she felt in her life. Kristin sometimes identified with me in the divorce, as daughters often do, and acted out some resentment toward Mark's new wife, despite their normally warm friendship. I knew that she loved her father and me, but she felt the same frustrations most teenagers do.

As I considered the best way to help her understand her own value, I decided on a seminar taught by a good friend of mine, Terry Warner, a psychologist from Provo, Utah. I wanted Kristin to learn about making responsible choices and about loving herself and others. After talking to Terry and assuring him (and perhaps myself) that Kristin's habit was not yet life threatening, I decided that Mark E., Kristin, and I would take the seminar together.

In my judgment, the seminar accomplished what I hoped it would. We talked at length after each one, and our already open relationship broadened as we discussed new ideas. Kristin and Mark E. learned more about themselves and their relationships. Kristin especially began to notice things about her friends and made astute observations about their behaviors and attitudes. I felt that she was moving in the right direction. I was very hopeful that she would be okay.

The month of April promised to be as frantic as the end of the school year usually is. Mark E.'s graduation was nearing, the roadshow would be performed during the last week of the month, and there were dozens of school-related activities at all three schools with Haroldsens in them.

Monday night of the last week in April of 1986 began with news of a tragedy. My friend Linda, who had faced many struggles with her family in recent years, lost her eldest son to suicide. A mutual friend called to tell me, and I was devastated.

In my life there were two things I most feared: a divorce and the loss of a child. I had faced one and survived it, but I always knew that the other would be too much to bear. My heart ached for Linda, and I immediately tried to call her. No one was home, so I kept trying to call, but by Tuesday morning I still hadn't gotten in touch with her.

Tuesday was going to be a "catch up at home day," so I called Linda off and on as I did laundry and ironing. While I ironed, I watched a daytime talk show. A guest began to tell the story of her bulimic daughter, which immediately caught my attention. I wasn't worrying about Kristin's situation on a constant basis; my feeling was that we had dealt with her problem, and I had no real reason to think that she was still making herself throw up. But I was not blind to the possibilities, and this particular story was my first realization of the potential of this disease.

The woman's daughter belonged to a college sorority where the girls taught each other about throwing up to maintain weight. They could eat all the pizza and ice cream they wanted and still fit into that dress on Saturday night. For some, it was just short-term weight control; it was not wise, but something they stopped doing with maturity. For others, the practice became a coping mechanism for their many stresses and then it became uncontrollable. One morning, the woman went to wake her daughter, who she thought had overslept, and she found that her daughter had died during the night.

It was the first time I realized that we were dealing with something that was potentially fatal, not just something that made young women sick. I wrote down everything they said to look for: dark circles under the eyes, bloodshot eyes, swollen glands that give a chipmunk look to the face, and calluses on their knuckles from scraping against their teeth when they stuck them down their throat. None of these symptoms were evident in Kristin, but I was anxious to talk to her about what I had learned.

When she finally arrived home from school, Kristin was with her younger sister and a friend. They went right upstairs, and I followed them to her room. I didn't want to single Kristin out in front of the others, so I sat all three girls down on the bed and talked to them.

"I saw the most disturbing thing on TV today," I said. I told the whole story of the mother whose daughter is dead and why she died. I asked

them, "Do you know anyone at school who is doing this? It's so dangerous!" They all denied any knowledge of bulimic behavior and insisted
that they thought it was "so gross." Even as I look in retrospect, their
denial was believable. I have since learned that even when our behaviors
are destructive, if we still think we are in control of them, it is easy to deny
that they exist.

That evening we were off to our various activities; it was our first
roadshow performance. Wednesday passed quickly. That evening, as I
watched all five of my children singing and dancing and laughing on
stage, I felt so blessed and happy.

Finally, on Thursday, I was determined to find Linda one way or
another. I decided to go to her mother's house. I discovered Linda was
at home; she just wasn't answering the phone. I went there and found
two other friends whom I also knew. We talked for a while together until
they left.

At last, Linda and I spoke alone and she told me about all the crosscur-
rents of her feelings: love, loss, anger, numbness, and disbelief. We talked
for a long time, and I knew that the thing I could offer was understanding
and a listening ear. I wanted to do something to help with the funeral the
next day. Linda said that several books on death had been suggested to
her and asked if I would pick them up at a bookstore. As I left to get my
children at school, I promised to find the books for her.

When I picked up the kids, Kristin was noticeably quiet. Davey's death
was especially hard on her for several reasons. Davey and Kristin were
the same age and had known each other since they were children. I also
believe that the death of a peer is harder for teenagers because it is so
abnormal. I had suggested that she and I visit Linda (Kristin's happy presence was nearly always a boost to others), but it just wasn't the right time
for her yet. I dropped Kristin and Nicky off at home.

I knew that if we were going to spend the quiet evening at home that
we were all looking forward to, I'd better get to a bookstore right away, so
I headed to the nearby mall. I got all the titles on the list and looked at a
few other books in the section on grief and death. A few were interesting,
so I added them, then, as an afterthought, I got a copy of each book for
myself. *If I read the same books*, I reasoned, *I'll be better able to talk with*

Linda and understand what she is feeling and learning. I didn't realize that I would need these same books later.

No one in our house felt like cooking dinner, so I stopped for chicken on the way home. Dinner was typical if a bit quieter than usual. All of us were aware of our friends' sorrow, but normal life has a way of popping in on grief. Later, Kristin's brother, Mark E., talked about noticing Kristin eating our meal in almost a frantic way. I did not see it, but the depth of her concern could easily have caused her to seek solace in food. We decided that the kids would all stay home and that we would watch TV together after homework and chores were finished.

I left the dishes to Nicky and Cammy and followed my thirteen-year-old, David, out to the backyard to mow the lawn. I wanted to tell him that he did indeed have to use the grass catcher whether it slowed the job or not.

As I stepped out to the yard, I noticed the beauty of my surroundings. We never know which moment will be the last one before our lives are changed irrevocably; mine was a moment of awareness and appreciation. The yard of this house was one of my favorite things about it. It was full of trees and had serenity to it. The house itself represented a milestone in my life. I had chosen and bought it by myself; it was clean and bright. The neighborhood and my own little piece of it were all I hoped they would be. The evening was full of the scent and promise of spring, my children were studying and working in beautiful and peaceful surroundings, and I was grateful for my life.

Suddenly, Kristin's voice shattered the cool evening air. From her bathroom window I heard her scream that she needed my help. I ran through the kitchen and up the stairs to her room. She was in the bathroom clutching her stomach. Her face was flushed and she looked terrified.

"What's the matter?" I shouted, trying to focus her attention on me.

"Oh Mom, I took some baking soda to make myself throw up and now I can't! I hurt so bad!"

I tried to help her without knowing one thing I could really do, and finally ran to phone the doctor. I got an answering service and the operator said that she would have the doctor call me back. I knew I couldn't wait, so I said, "Nevermind, I'll take her straight to the hospital."

As I dashed out of the house, I tried to think of all the bases that needed covering for the hour or so we would be gone. I asked Mark E. to take the younger children to their Dad's and tell him that Kristin was sick and I was taking her to the doctor. I also thought that maybe Linda would like to read that evening, so I also asked him to take her the books. I helped Kristin to the car, wondering how to talk to her without making her feel worse. Maybe this would be the thing that would help her learn.

There was a lot of traffic and construction on the main road near our street, so I decided to take Kristin to an emergency clinic nearby rather than the long route to the hospital. I assumed that the clinic was a smaller version of a hospital emergency room. It turned out to be more of an advanced first aid station. For stitches or a simple fracture it would be fine, but the sympathetic staff had no idea what to do in this situation.

"You'll have to take her to the hospital," they said. "We don't have anything here to help her."

They had her lie down while they called ahead to the hospital. In the fifteen minutes since she had ingested the baking soda, Kristin's stomach had swollen to the size of a small watermelon, and she had to unzip the denim skirt she was wearing.

Evidently, no one had noticed that the swelling had happened mostly in the few minutes since our arrival, because a nurse suddenly asked, "Could you be pregnant?" In spite of her pain, Kristin laughed out loud at the idea of suddenly noticing that she was pregnant. But she did suddenly notice something else.

"Mom, I can't feel my legs!"

All the circulation to her legs had been cut off and we had to put her in a wheelchair to get her back in the car to rush to the hospital. All the way to the hospital we repeated the same conversation, both of us worrying about the other's pain.

"Oh, Kristin, why didn't you tell me you were still having trouble with throwing up?"

Kristin's reply over and over was, "I am so sorry; I'll never do it again. I never thought anything would happen to me. I hurt so bad!"

Within ten minutes we were pulling up to the emergency room of the hospital. I ran in for a wheelchair and dashed back out to get Kristin. The trauma team was waiting and took her right into the trauma unit in the ER. No one knew what to do. Until that moment, I suppose, I had felt that once I finally found the right place to take her, my daughter would be fine.

There was no such place.

The experienced and concerned staff had simply never seen anything like her condition. I signed all the admitting papers.

Kristin's pain was so intense that they finally gave her a shot of morphine and she was able to relax. I also felt a sense of relief that she was no longer in such intense pain. After exploring all possible options, the doctors inserted a needle into her stomach to relieve some pressure, and she was able to feel her legs again. It was not possible to pump her stomach because the reaction of the ingested soda with the acid in her stomach was so quick that her esophagus was completely closed off.

In the years since this happened, I am often asked if I felt Kristin could have been saved if this or that thing had been done, or if I had gone right to the hospital. A nurse who was present that evening later told a friend of mine that the moments spent at the clinic were disastrous for Kristin's treatment. Kristin's father, Mark, has struggled with feelings of resentment and anger that she was not saved.

But I was there. I saw what was done and the urgency with which it was done. I saw men and women trying with all their store of knowledge and experience to save this young life. The internal damage Kristin suffered had happened almost immediately, and I've wondered since if the next hours might have been for the sake of our adjustment. I do know that my feelings toward the medical people who tried to help her are feelings of appreciation.

Finally, I realized that I needed to let someone know what was going on. My friends were my support network, so they were the ones I thought of first. I called Jane, a dear friend and neighbor, and Barbara, a new friend who had helped me with the roadshow. Jane and I had a doctor friend in common, and I asked her to ask him if he felt there was a particular specialist who could help Kristin. She promised to check, and I told her that I would call if anything changed. My conversation with Barbara was much the same, and I closed with the same promise. The next thing

I knew, both of them were walking through the emergency room doors.

Shortly after their arrival, Kristin's dad burst through the doors. He was frantic. He had been trying to locate us and I had not yet remembered to call him and let him know where we were going. When we had left the house a nightmare ago, I wasn't sure where we were headed, and since the urgency had escalated, I hadn't thought clearly. The little group of us—Mark, Jane, Barbara, and I—kept going back and forth from the trauma unit where we held Kristin's hand and kissed her forehead to the waiting room where we bolstered each other. The doctors continued to try different things. Late Thursday evening a specialist, Dr. Layton Aldredge, was called in. As soon as he arrived, he said that surgery was an absolute necessity. Even then, no one knew how much could be repaired or what the final damage would be.

As the gurney was wheeled down the hall to the operating room, I kissed her and said jokingly, "Don't you dare die! I love you."

"I won't," she said. "I love you, too."

David Letterman was wisecracking in the background, although no one was paying any attention. Even now, I am reminded of that night whenever I hear him. As funny as he may be, those minutes were the ones in which I first faced the possibility that I could lose Kristin. I kept saying and thinking, "What if she dies? How can I survive without Kristin?"

As my eldest daughter with the ability to light up our home, she was too much a part of our life to be gone. Over and over I repeated, "I don't think I can live without her." My wise friend Jane responded each time, "You don't have to carry that suitcase now. She's going to live." I realized that it was true; I should only have had to carry the baggage I'd been handed so far. At first, I knew that my daughter was in pain and we needed help. At the clinic I realized it was more serious than pain and a simple procedure, and in the intervening hours I had begun to realize that Kristin could be sick for a long time. For now, I would carry only what I had to.

Besides, we all knew that she would live. My comment to her on the way to surgery was made only to ease tension. Her death was unthinkable!

After a few hours in surgery, Dr. Aldredge came to the waiting room and sat down on a desk. "We almost lost her a couple of times," he said, "But she's strong and healthy. The damage to her organs is extensive, involving her kidneys, liver, and pancreas. We had to remove part of her large and small intestine. In the morning, we'll have to go back in and remove her stomach, but she wouldn't have survived more surgery tonight."

It was a lot to absorb, and I spent the rest of the night trying to make the adjustments my mind needed to make. From singing and dancing and laughing on a stage one night to being so sick that her body would never work well again, Kristin's life was changed forever.

Early in the morning, I made two very difficult calls. I called my mom and dad to tell them that I was at the hospital with Kristin and that I did not know if she would live. I will always regret that I did not call my parents the night before so that they could have been with us. But I never thought it was life or death, and I knew that Mom and Dad would have worried all night. Then I called Linda to tell her that I would not be able to attend Davey's funeral because I was at the hospital with Kristin and the outcome was uncertain. All I could do in both calls was relay the information—any more conversation was impossible.

Friday morning, the hospital began to fill with family and friends. I had made two phone calls the day before and the word had spread to dozens of adults and teenagers who loved us all. I can't begin to recall each one, but their presence was heartening.

The next step in this bizarre journey came as the doctor brought grave news. In the movies, when the doctor says, "We can't get a brain reading," it means that there will have to be a real miracle for the patient to get better. When I received that news, I thought, *Oh no, not brain damage too!* Despite what I told my mom, I was still not seriously considering that my child would die. When a nurse asked me if I would sign some forms donating Kristin's eyes and any other undamaged parts, I said, "Of course." But I thought, *Why can't you wait to see if she dies?*

Then, as I sat on her bed, I began to understand that Kristin was no longer alive. She was being kept technically alive by machines, but she was no longer there. After all the surgery and blood transfusions from the night before, Kristin's body was swollen and cold. She did not look like the Kristin I knew.

As I sat beside her, feeling like I was going to die too, I silently cried out in pain. At that moment, I knew, without question, that there is a Father in Heaven and that He loves us. I knew that He loved Kristin and would care for her. I knew that He loved me and would sustain me. I knew that if He loved Kristin and me, then He loved every person on earth. I know that is true every time I say it or think about it. There was peace about Kristin's death from that moment on. I was able to accept the unacceptable.

Mark came into the intensive care unit and said, "Lois, we need to talk about turning off the life support systems. She could go on like this for weeks." We agreed that he should go make the arrangements to have the machines discontinued. Just as he turned to go, the digital machine measuring the struggling heart began to slow down.

"Wait, Mark, come back. She's dying."

We watched as the monitor registered her quiet passing. From seventy-two beats a minute, the machine slowly decreased to zero, and she was gone. I kissed her goodbye and left the ICU.

As I entered the hall of the hospital, I felt fragile and transparent. Looking down the hall at all those people who loved us was like looking through the wrong end of a telescope. Everyone looked small and distant, and I could not comprehend anything. The hospital was overflowing with friends and family who had appeared for support as word spread through the community. I saw an intimate friend; I knew that I knew her well, but I did not recognize her until she hugged me.

There were fifty or sixty teenagers weeping in each other's arms. Everyone wanted to hug and comfort me and receive comfort from knowing that I was OK, but I was unable to respond. I know that my mother and father and sister were there, but I don't remember where. I could not focus on anything or give comfort to anyone. Some images are clear, others fuzzy; all are distorted. I remember making my way through the throng of people and appreciating the compassion without really feeling it.

Someone from the hospital staff said, "Who do you want to take care of the funeral?"

I don't want to have a funeral! I wanted to shout.

But Stephen Wade, a close friend, knew a mortuary he felt was good, so the decision was made.

Then they wanted to know where I wanted to have her buried. Again my mind screamed, *I don't want to have her buried!*

Stephen told me where their family plots were and I thought, *I would love to be buried by the Wades*, and that decision was taken care of. I was so ill-equipped to make decisions about the funeral and burial of my sixteen-year-old daughter. Her father was no better off, and we did not know how to help each other.

Finally and reluctantly, I entered the elevator with my children—Mark E., David, Nicky, and Cammy—but the elevator felt empty. It seemed that getting on that elevator to leave was like accepting that she was gone. If I were to stay there, she would stay too. All the love and concern and prayers in that hospital were like my own life support system, and I did not want to cut it off.

A friend whose husband had died once told me that she felt as if she were wrapped in cotton during those first hours and days. I felt that way as well, and I have come to believe that it is not only shock, as many believe, but the loving arms of the Holy Spirit, giving our minds and spirits time to absorb the sadness before grief and then healing begin.

When I got home, I went straight to Kristin's room. I wanted to be with her things, to be in the place she had left expecting to return to in a matter of hours. It felt like being with her things was a little bit like being with her. The stream of visitors that would flow for days began right away.

One friend came upstairs, and we sat on the floor talking. I felt her love and sympathy, but it was also the beginning of an important realization for me. People who lose a child rarely want to avoid talking about their loss. In fact, there is real comfort in the telling and retelling of even painful details. I heard many stories and shared mine over and over in the next months. I continue to feel a bond with parents who have lost children.

The constant stream of visitors continued, most of them bearing desserts. Everyone wanted to do something—food is the traditional balm and dessert is something we can put together right away. With all the seriousness around me, I had to smile at the abundance of sugar in my kitchen. One friend came in with a pie, and I looked blankly at her.

"You don't know who I am, do you, Lois?" she said. "I'm Joan Wilde."

I knew Joan well. It was surreal to see someone I knew and not recognize her.

Someone said I had to write an obituary. Impossible! I couldn't think
to put two words together, let alone write about the death of my daughter.
Catherine Pedersen, who had stayed at the house, sat down at the typewriter in the kitchen and wrote an obituary. At the time I could not say
that Kristin had an eating disorder, so she wrote the cause as "extreme
stomach disorder."

Then there was another decision to make. What would Kristin wear
in her coffin? People say that there is comfort in making all the decisions
that go with a death. It wasn't so for me. Each time I had to decide something, I could look to a caring friend for advice and support.

Catherine came to my aid again. She had just bought a new white
eyelet nightgown that she said I could have. A nightgown sounded perfect
and comforting. I was so grateful to have someone make suggestions that
made the decisions easy. I did not want to think about details.

In an ideal world, a husband, wife, and children would pull together
and give comfort to each other in this kind of tragedy. Ours is a lovely
world, but it is not the ideal one. I've learned that even the strongest of
families and marriages can be threatened and destroyed by the trials of
life. In fact, in a time of loss, people who love each other often pull away
a bit at first and deal with the immediate emotions in their own way. That
was the case with our family.

For the next couple of days, we touched occasionally and briefly, and
then each found their own comfort. Perhaps it is too much to expect
several people who feel the same pain to be able to comfort each other.
The kids stayed mostly at Mark's, and all of them wanted to go back to
school. David and some friends went to Mill Valley and painted a rock
with the words, "Goodbye, Kristin, we'll miss you."

Cammy and Nicky remember sleeping on the trampoline at their dad's
with several friends. This gave the girls the time they needed to be the
focus of attention, to talk about their feelings, and to be away from the
constant solemnity of our house.

A friend later asked me if I wished I had been able to gather my children together and talk and teach them about life and death during those

first days. I am not a person plagued by regret about most things, but even more, I've learned that we were all where we could receive the most comfort. We can only give to each other what we have inside, and I had only a numbed heart for days.

After the funeral we did pull together, and my children's normal needs and views of life were essential for me. Before Kristin's death and in the years since, a hallmark characteristic of our family is that we talk. We talk a lot and about many things. Those days before the funeral were a blur for me, but none of us was left without comfort during that time.

Saturday afternoon before the funeral, Mark and I went together to choose a casket and headstone. It was sunny and warm, but my cocoon kept me from feeling much of anything, good or bad. I had always felt that anything would do to bury a person in and that it was foolish to spend a lot on a box in the ground. But when it comes to burying a loved one, it feels nicer to buy something pretty. We chose an aqua casket from the medium price range and a bronze headstone with lilies of the valley around the edges.

We chose a burial site for her, and I bought the one next to it for me. I felt the need to be sure I would be near her again, and that decision seemed to ensure that I would. People have to do these things every day, but it must always seem bizarre when caskets and burial plots are purchased for children and spouses and parents who were talking and laughing just hours before.

Sometime the evening of the day Kristin died, I began to think about the kids at Cottonwood High School. Even as I was feeling numb about most aspects of life, I felt urgency about communicating with her classmates. I wanted them to know that I had faith and that I was OK. I had already discovered something about our tragedy.

Because the circumstances were so unusual, there was media coverage right away. Many friends and strangers knew what had happened within hours or days. One friend later told me that she was so horrified by Kristin's death that she was afraid to see me. She just knew that I would be a devastated ghost of myself.

"When I saw you," she said, "I felt better because I saw that you were drawing on some resources I wasn't aware of." I was devastated, but my experience at Kristin's bedside had never left me. I felt God's presence and comfort, and I wanted the high school students to feel a bit of it too.

The funeral had been set for 1:00 p.m. Monday, and school was to be dismissed for the service. I wanted her friends to come to the church with a sense of hope rather than despair. I decided that I would write a message to them and ask the PTA president to read it Monday morning over the PA system. While I thought several times about what I wanted to say, I just couldn't get it down on paper. By Sunday afternoon I had begun to think that maybe I would talk to the students myself.

Mark and I had agreed to ask Stephen Wade to speak at the funeral. Kristin had been a regular babysitter for the Wades for several years. She and Marcia, Steve's wife, knew each other well, and Kristin had felt like a member of the Wade family. We felt comfortable having him address Kristin's friends and ours. Steve came over and took me for a drive while we talked about the things I wanted him to say. I mentioned my decision to talk to the high school students, and he offered to pick me up Monday morning and drive me there.

Sunday night was the viewing, another step in my acceptance and grieving. We went earlier as a family to see Kristin's body and to decide whether to have the casket open or closed. The moment we saw the body the decision was obvious: this body did not look anything like Kristin. Kristin's very essence was one of life and excitement—her appearance exuded her personality. Her hair and makeup were light and airy with lots of natural color and beauty. But this body was still swollen and puffy, graying, and pasty. Her hair had a stiff, artificial look. Instead of being upset by her appearance, I felt better. What I was looking at was a container that used to hold Kristin's spirit and now was just an empty box. I was unable to imagine how I would bury my daughter; now I realized that we do not bury the person, just the body. That realization made the next two days easier.

I arrived at the mortuary about fifteen minutes early for the viewing, and there were already people lined up waiting to see our family. It was raining and cold, but people came to offer and receive comfort. We had placed a beautiful portrait of Kristin on an easel near the casket. For about four hours, people filed past and we laughed and wept and hugged and remembered. For me, it was an important part of the process. I gained tremendous strength from those who came.

Monday morning Steve took me to the school. The principal, Mr. Bergstrom, greeted us warmly and kindly. He is one of the most thoughtful people I've ever known, and he expressed his sympathy and shock at my loss. He said that the whole school was shocked on Friday at the news of Kristin's death. He thought it would be a good idea for the whole student body to hear from me. He and I were both aware that a faint rumor of suicide had circulated, and we both wanted the kids to know the real story.

He introduced me over the PA system that broadcasts to each room of the school. I took the phone receiver that is connected to the system and my voice sounded odd, like it belonged to someone else. But the words were from my heart.

I can't remember all I said, but I did give them a brief version of what had happened Thursday night. Then I talked about the importance of knowing who they are and not focusing on their looks. I briefly mentioned the danger involved in unwise weight attitudes. Mostly I wanted them to know that I knew that if it were right for Kristin to be alive, she would be. I felt it was her time to go. I expressed my love for them and said that I was at peace.

Steve and I left the building, and as we reached the car, I glanced at the seminary building. In a Salt Lake City high school, there will be a significant number of students in seminary during any period, and I wondered if the PA system had been turned on in there. We decided to check, and it had not been on. The seminary principal asked if I would address his students, too. The three classes were gathered together (I knew I could do it one more time, but I doubted if I had the strength to deliver my message three times).

I repeated what I had told the rest of the school, only this time it was easier because I could see their response. Their eyes filled with tears, but I felt they were tears of empathy and sensitivity, not anguish. I felt even more comfortable expressing my faith with this group right before me because we shared the same faith. I repeated to them my plea that any of them experiencing the symptoms Kristin had to confide in someone. I left feeling satisfied that I accomplished what I'd hoped to.

Steve drove me home to get ready for the funeral, but I seemed to have used up my store of energy. I couldn't think about clothes, and the blouse I had worn to the viewing had mascara on the shoulder. Once again, a dear friend came to the rescue. Jane Pugh took the blouse to a dry cleaner and had it back in time to get ready to go to the church.

The funeral was beautiful, but I felt like I was not really present. The chapel and gymnasium were full all the way to the back. I was not really aware of the number of people until friends told me later that it was close to one thousand people. It was amazing to me how many people knew Kristin and loved her. She touched many lives and had made a difference to them during her sixteen and a half years, and her death had also touched many who barely knew her.

Many, many friends went to the cemetery with the family. My father dedicated the grave, and after a few minutes I felt it was time for me to go. But no one wanted to leave. It could be that they had the same hesitations I had felt Friday at the hospital: leaving meant it was really over. I began circulating, hugging and talking with everyone. I felt like everybody's mother. I hoped that by getting up I would signal that it was time to go, but no one followed that lead. Finally, after about an hour, I decided to go, leaving many friends at the grave.

A part of my life was over. I had four great children and a life I was grateful for. I felt the comfort of a promise of eternal life. But losing this child, if only for the relatively short spell of mortality, had extinguished a spark in me that I wasn't sure I could ever rekindle. I went home to begin a different life.

For nearly three decades since her death, I have guided thousands to rebuild hope in shattered lives. Through avenues from special victims' assistance to public speaking and private counseling, I have utilized my personal experience, formal education, and professional practice in pursuit of peace and wholeness for my clients.

After surviving the devastation of Kristin's death and the end of my fourteen-year marriage to the father of our five children, I found meaning in my losses by helping others to prevent and heal similar wounds. Since 1986, I have been addressing multiple aspects of relational traumas. I have gone from thinking I'd be working on eating disorders to helping people heal from relational trauma. My life has prepared me for anything. I'm happy, and I credit my faith in Christ for that.

CHAPTER 4

writings

*Today I talked to Deborah about me throwing up after I eat. I know I
need to stop. I made her promise not to tell anyone but in a way I hope
she does because I know I need the help.*

—excerpt from Kristin's journal

I had a hard time reading that after Kris died. As young teenage girls, we
write a lot of things in our "private" journals about how we feel and what
we are going through. Kris was just like any other teenage girl, and she
kept a journal pretty regularly for years. She had the normal entries, such
as "My sibling is driving me crazy," "Why doesn't this boy like me?", "My
parents don't understand me," and "I hate school."

As I read through her journals, I realized they weren't much different
than mine, besides that Kris didn't really know what she wanted and was
constantly changing depending on whom she was around at the time.
I knew at times she wasn't happy with the way she looked, which isn't
much different than any other teenage girl except that every time Kris
looked into the rearview mirror, she felt fat. We are hard on ourselves; I
wish that she knew how beautiful she was. There was so much more to
her than her looks, yet in many cases that was all she saw.

When teenagers write in their journals, they feel like they are putting
down on paper what they did that day as well as their thoughts and
feelings that no one else will read. I know there are many experiences
that Kris wouldn't have wanted me to share. Others involved in those

experiences also wouldn't have wanted me to share them—like I mentioned in an earlier chapter, I felt like my life would now be an open book because what Kristin and I did, we did together. Many of those experiences were in her journals. It has stirred up a lot of emotions for me.

I remember having that conversation with Kris and telling her that I wouldn't tell anyone. It didn't seem like a big deal. It couldn't be life threatening—you just eat and throw up, and it sounds pretty harmless. I wasn't going to tell anyone because that's what friends at that age do—they keep each other's secrets. Now, being older and looking back, I wonder what would have happened if I had said something and if I really could have made a difference.

I know it would help many of you to see what she thought and felt and what she was going through, but for the most part her experiences expressed in the private journals were that of a normal teenage girl. I finally decided to keep most of her journals just that: "private." It wasn't worth bringing up the things that happened in the past. I did choose to add a few of her entries to show that Kristin was looking toward the future and wanted to have children and that she enjoyed celebrating birthdays, dating boys, and doing crazy high school things. She was normal with normal thoughts; she was just trying to figure out who she was and who she wanted to be. During that process she had body issues and felt fat, and she didn't know how to process that in a healthy way. Her struggles combined with general ignorance resulted in her eating what she wanted and then making herself throw up.

KRISTIN'S JOURNAL ENTRIES

LOOKING TOWARD THE FUTURE

Nov 26, 1984

Wow, I am writing two days in a row. Well, today was pretty well and horrid! I don't know, I guess Mondays usually are. All morning I was so tired. I thought I was going to die of boredom right in school, but I didn't. All of my days seem to be medium, and I feel like I just need something to look forward to—anything, anything at all. I am looking forward to getting married. Fat chance, huh? Fat: that is me. I feel so fat; I am so fat.

Mom keeps saying I will get anorexic if I lose more weight, but if I will, I am only fifteen and never been kissed. Joking! I could have, but only a couple of times—the guys just weren't for me. A lot of girls would have I bet! When I grow up (I sound like a six-year-old), I want three to five kids, and I think a girl named Laura Ashley and another one—oh, I can't remember! Oh, well. Maybe tomorrow will bring something better. (To my kids, if I ever have any.)

WHO AM I?

December 7, 1984

Well, it is almost Christmas and today was OK. I guess this whole week I have been the biggest spaz. I feel like I have to act like I "used to be." Some people don't like me because they say I am no fun anymore. I have a lot more fun when I spaz, but it's almost like it's a fake front. People always say you'll go through stages where you'll have to "find yourself," and I feel like that's how I am right now—I don't really know who I am.

FUN TIMES AND FRIENDSHIP

March 21, 1986

Today was OK I suppose. After school, Deborah and I went to my dad's. He said we were having a party and to bring a friend. Well, we got there and it was a cleaning party. The den was really dusty and hadn't ever been cleaned. Actually, it was fun. The music was cranked up, and we all had certain areas to clean. At first I hated it, but it got better and we just danced around and sang and dusted. The relationship Deb and I have is cool. I wish sometimes we could move out of our houses and get an apartment together. I think we could do it, but it would probably only last for a few days. We spend so much time together; we have fun.

KRISTIN ADMITS TO THROWING UP

April 6, 1986

Today I got up at like 10:00 a.m., and I went downstairs and listened to a talk on tape. Then around 1:00 p.m., Deborah, Monica, Amy, Patti, and I went downtown. It was kind of fun. We parked at the mall and were walking around the stores. I wanted these earrings, so Monica got them for me. When I got home, William and Tony were there and I talked to them for a while. I think William's thinking about me again. Not to be stuck up, but I really do think he likes me. But I don't know. On my way home it was funny because Monica was spazzing out and Deborah was kind of getting mad, but then once we got on the private roads she was OK. I was laughing so hard, and Monica was out the sunroof. It was so fun I was dying. Then after a while when I had been home and William and Tony had gone, Monica came over and then William also came over. He was being really cool to me. Deborah came over for a second. She was sad because her parents wouldn't let her do anything. I felt bad for her— Monica and I just talked to the guys all night. Then they left, and I stayed up with two of my brothers' friends that were over. I ate a ton of food and then threw up. It is the *worst* habit now. I throw up about every day. Duh! I probably should stop soon, huh?

KRISTIN'S LAST JOURNAL ENTRY

April 20, 1986

For some reason, all day today I've felt like it should be Thursday, but it is not. After school, I had singing and then a play practice for church. I had so much fun! I was spazin' so bad I think everyone was embarrassed by me. But I had fun! This guy that goes to junior high school is about the cutest. Annette and Marianne know him. He's in eighth grade and is too cute. I can't even handle it, and he's so much younger. Duh, Kristin, you're practically three years older. Now I feel dumb because my mom came home and said that Annette introduced him to her and he said, "Yeah, Kristin took my headband and won't give it back." I can hardly believe I am even thinking about him. I wish he were my age. It doesn't matter; he would probably hate me. Well anyway, I had a blast! Deborah and I went on stage to accept our award, and we made the biggest fools of ourselves—who cares! Nanette's little brother was with Trevor. He is a doll also. He said Nanette had to go to the hospital today and run some tests. I am kind of worried. I really miss her. She was too cute, and I hope she's OK!

Many people loved and adored Kristin and were impacted in many ways. A few of her friends wanted to remember her in a small tribute. I have included several here to show their love, grief, and joy in the time that they spent by her side.

WENDY W. D.

I remember when I heard that she had passed away. I was so sad, and I also remember thinking that I didn't know that someone could die from this. She was always very sweet to me, even though I didn't hang out with her outside of school.

MARK HEDGEPATH

I found out when I arrived later in the day, when I went to her mom's house to hang out with Mark, one of my best friends. I enjoyed being in that home because of how kind Lois was. She was devastated by the news, and the whole family followed solemnly. I'm saddened because I had no idea that Kristin was fighting bulimia. She was cute and beautiful. The love we felt for her then continues on today. She is missed.

ROBYN BEMIS SMITH

I will never forget the feeling walking through the halls after the announcement was made that she had died—silence with tears. I was so shocked I just couldn't say anything at all. I may be wrong, but it seemed like everyone just left and went home. Kristin had the gift of looking into your eyes when she was listening to you talk. She gave you the impression that nothing else mattered at that moment. What you said was important. I wish we had all the technology back then to hear that laugh of hers. That is what was confusing about her death. She loved people and had such a *deep* laugh. Her smile was easy and she was always positive. How did she not see herself as absolutely beautiful? I never would have put her in the category of self-doubt. Of course, when we were sixteen, we didn't have the insight we have now.

When I was older, I taught high school health. Of course, we covered eating disorders. I really didn't know how I was going to get through it until that day to teach it came. I had handouts with the story from the newspaper and other pictures of Kristin. I knew I had to talk about her. I had to tell her story. I had to make sure my kids knew what an impact her death had on everyone. My eyes were not dry, and I felt such a different connection with my students those days. They were silent and listened like never before. They agreed on how beautiful she was. They were confused as to why.

The follow-up lesson was always how we can be more aware of the feelings of people around us, be nice to people, get to know people, and ask questions so that this *never, ever* happens again. Through the next many years of teaching, I shared Kristin's story with various girls that I suspected of having eating disorders. They listened well and had many questions about her. It never got any easier to talk about her death, but I knew I had to share it. I think my students felt it was "real talk." They could feel my sadness, and I know it stuck with them. Kids can understand information, but when you touch their emotions, it becomes real. It was always worth it. Kristin is always worth it.

MARGO WILSON LYBBERT

I will never forget that day. I was at Bonneville Junior High and got called down to the office for my mom to tell me the horrible news. Kristin's sister, Nicky, was my best friend, and I still remember the look of hurt on her face when I saw her that day. We walked into Kristin's room and just sat in her bed together. I love the Haroldsen family, and they will always be family to me.

DEBI LARSEN SAGER

I was in Mr. Garret's physiology class when the announcement came over the loud speaker. Everyone was in disbelief. After class, I remember the feeling in the halls—eerily quiet, somber, very heavy with sorrow and sadness. Then we all started talking about our memories of Kristin. Nothing but good was said about her. She was the kindest, sweetest, most nonjudgmental person I have ever met in my life. She was a friend to everyone.

A few weeks before Kristin's death, another friend of ours, Rebecca

Bowden, had passed away in a car accident. Kristin went with me to her funeral and was an incredible comfort to me. I will never forget the kindness and support she gave me on that day. It's so sad that we had to go through it all again so soon after with Kristin. Both girls were too young to pass from this earth, and both are now angels looking down upon us. One thing I will never forget about Kristin was her contagious smile. She lit up the room!

I've told Kristin's story in various lessons I've taught over the years, hoping that something good will come out of her passing. Let us never forget her and her spirit.

HARVEY LARSON

My locker was on the exact opposite side of Kristin's. She was always so happy and always smiling. That day brings back so many memories. I do not recall the class I was in when the news over the intercom came out, but hearing that news was just so incredibly unbelievable. The hallways were so quiet the rest of the day. The silence, the tears—a high school gone so quiet.

ROWDY BELLIS

Kristin was one of my favorites! The nicest, most beautiful young lady *inside and out*. Who knew that someone so wonderful, so beautiful, and so liked by everyone was having questions about self-esteem. The day before, I was goofing off after school in the halls with Jeff S., Steph, and Kristin. Little did I know that would be the last time that I would see that infectious smile! When I heard the news I was in a state of shock. So sad. I couldn't believe our friend was gone. Kristin will never be forgotten; she touched so many people in a positive way. Hope this book can help others, too.

BECKY MCQUEEN BROWN

I remember when she passed away; it was such a sad time for all involved.

NICK DELAND

I didn't go to the hospital, but I remember hearing the news when I arrived at Cottonwood High School the next morning. I remember Kristen from junior high and high school. It was such a horrible tragedy. I remember how blown away we all were when we heard of her unfortunate passing. She was such a nice person. I hope her story of her struggles with bulimia will help and inspire others.

CATHERINE PEDERSEN, DEBORAH'S MOTHER

It's been twenty-eight years since Kristin's death, and yet in many ways, it seems like only yesterday. Because of the impact of her death on our family, we will never forget it. I remember the shock of the news the evening that Mark Haroldsen came to our home. We didn't sleep much that evening because we were so deeply concerned for Kristin and her family and also for our daughter, Deborah.

The next morning, as we hurried to the high school and then to the hospital, a huge lump was stuck in my throat. It all seemed so unreal! Kristin was always the one who lit up the room with an exuberant zest for life. She was so much fun to be around!

As we entered the hospital area where Kristin was, the mood was somber. We weren't exactly sure of Kristin's status until Deborah and I were invited to go in and see her. I didn't stay long; it was painful to see her so bloated. I knew in my heart that it would probably take a miracle for her to recover. We kept praying and hoping for that miracle, but it was not meant to be. It was heartbreaking.

Then the practical side of me took over, and I was asking what I could do to help. I remembered that I had just received a package in the mail. It was a beautiful, flowing, long white eyelet nightgown that I had seen in a catalog. I had never worn it, and I thought it would be perfect for Kristin to be buried in.

Lois, Kristin's mother and a very good friend and neighbor of ours, was in a fog. She was having a difficult time making decisions. I put my arms around her and assured her that we were there to help her in any way that we could. None of us could possibly be prepared for the awkward time after the death of a child.

My heart went out to Nicky (Kristin's younger sister), and I offered to take her home. We talked and then I let her lie down for a while before I took her back to the busyness of her own home. When we returned to Lois's home, I told Lois about the beautiful nightgown. She seemed grateful that I was helping her to make some important decisions. She then said that we needed to write Kristin's obituary, so I sat down at the typewriter and together we wrote it. It was an honor because of our deep love for Kristin and her family.

I am grateful for the opportunity to remember the precious (and sometimes mischievous) escapades of Deborah and Kristin and all of their many friends. There was so much support and love for Kristin at her funeral. I wish that she had realized that she could have reached out to any of us. It's up to us to be more aware and to reach out to give each other hope and love.

All of this time since her death, I look back and see how Kristin's life and others have influenced my own life. After her death, I studied bulimia and I became more aware of its effects and devastation on families. Because we had four daughters and four sons, I wanted to understand this disease and also help our own children deal with the loss of Kristin. I don't believe we could have been as positive and understanding without our faith in God. It helped us to see the eternal plan and know that we would be with Kristin again in the future.

I have learned to have great empathy for others, and maybe it all started with my love, caring, and understanding for our dear Kristin Haroldsen.

MY (DEBORAH'S) JOURNAL ENTRY

THE DAY AFTER KRIS DIED

May 3, 1986

Today was weird. I am not sure what to think or feel. I had to be at the mortuary at 10:00 a.m. to meet Lois and Mark to show them the nightgown that my mom had for Kris to wear. Then Monica and I went to ZCMI to get a slip for her to wear under the nightgown. I have had a cold feeling inside of me all day. I feel alone, and I am really sad. Yet I don't believe it is true. I keep thinking that she is just going to come walking into my house any minute. It is really hard for me. I am really scared. I keep thinking I see her and I feel her and I have these scary dreams—it is really hard for me to explain. I feel super lonely and super sad.

I had several friends come over and bring a sympathy card for me to sign for Lois. We (Steph and Jenny) went to lunch at McDonald's and we saw Dana there. My feelings started all over again; it was really hard.

I came back home to try and get some sleep. Several of the girls from church (Annette, Maryann, Janelle, Rachael) came over to visit me. I am fine until I see someone, and it makes me sad all over again. I get sick of people calling me.

I didn't know what to do and I couldn't sleep, so I drove over to Kristin's and picked up Nicky, her sister. We drove up the canyon and saw the big rock that was painted by David and his friends. They had painted, "We'll miss you, Kris!" on the rock. Right when I saw it, I looked at Nicky, and we both started crying again. We drove to her dad's house and just sat around and talked to the family. We looked at old photos. A friend of their family, Dick H., had planted a tree at her mom and dad's house in memory of Kris. He said it would bloom at the same time every year to remember Kris. Nicky and I left and got a Diet Coke just like Kris and I always did. We stopped by my house and picked up all the posters of photos that I made for Kris to set out at the funeral, and we took them to Lois's house. I stayed there until late and finally came home knowing I need to try and get some sleep. So sad—that's me.

THE DAY OF THE VIEWING

May 4, 1986

This morning I didn't want to go to church, so I slept most of the morning and then went over for the very end. I felt OK this morning, but the second that I stepped into the church I was rushed full of memories and I started to cry. All of church was about Kris and everyone talked about her and shared memories of her. I had the worst headache. I need to stop crying, but can't. I went over to the Haroldsen's, and we loaded the cars with things of Kris's we wanted to take to the viewing. We then all drove over to the mortuary. Lois and Mark had planned on it being an open casket. We all walked in and there she was lying in the casket. It was the first time that I had seen her since leaving the hospital. They had her in the white nightgown from my mother. I walked slowly over to the casket and looked at her. I was shocked. I couldn't recognize her at all. She was still very swollen and bloated. After the family saw her, they felt like it would be best to have a closed casket. I was so happy and thought it was the best decision. I was kind of looking forward to seeing her all day, but it made me even sadder when it didn't look like my best friend. Oh, Kris, I miss you.

The family told me I could stand in the line with them by the casket; I was just going through motions now. I probably shouldn't have since all I did was cry. Each time I saw someone I knew, the tears would start all over. I finally left at about 9:30 p.m.

THE DAY OF THE FUNERAL

May 5, 1986

After my mother wrote the obituary for the Haroldsens, the family got together and planned out the funeral and made all the arrangements. Mark, her father, asked me if I would speak at the funeral and represent her friends. My immediate reaction was, "Yes, of course I will." But then he followed with, "We really want you to talk, but we don't know if you can without being so emotional."

The morning of the funeral, the church was packed. There were so many people there, and I remember just shaking—my hands and stomach were a mess. While people were still in where the viewing was taking place, I went to the bathroom and locked myself in a stall. I just prayed to my Father in Heaven and to Kris to help me say what I wanted to say, and I told her I needed her to help me to get through it without being so emotional. I walked back in with the family. They had the family prayer and we proceeded together, following behind Kristin's casket into the main hall where the funeral was taking place. The family all sat down on the front rows, and I followed her dad up on the stand. I didn't look out at all the people—so many people were there. The walls were lined and the seats were all taken. I had my head down most of the time just listening, but I was a mess and couldn't stop crying. I was next to speak and just kept thinking, *Kris, you have got to help me.* I stood up at the pulpit and in that second, I was calm. My tears were gone and I looked down and was able to read and say what I had prepared without any emotion. The second I finished, I lost it. I was comforted knowing that Kris was with me; at that moment, she was by my side.

———————————————

To this day, I know that is the only way that I could have gotten through it.

At her funeral, I shared an analogy about how life is like a train ride: we all get on the train at different times and ride along together. We meet new friends and share experiences together. Some of us have to get off the train early and at different stops along the way, but we will all meet up together in the end.

I want to believe that Kris got off the train a little early and that we will be together again, and my faith helps me believe that. I couldn't have gotten through all that I have been through without my faith in God and without Kris by my side.

CHAPTER 5

impact

I remember the morning of Kris's funeral. I was on my way to the church, and I had the radio on. The radio host made a comment saying, "Someone famous must have died today," and she went on to talk about the funeral that was taking place for the young girl that recently died from bulimia. At that moment, I realized how many people had already been impacted by Kris's death and that there was no way that I would be able to know how many more would be impacted in the future.

Everyone close to her was impacted by this event in a different way. Each of her siblings wanted to share his or her account with you.

MARK E.'S STORY

It was May 1, 1986, and my sister Kristin and I were hanging out in the kitchen after school as I enviously watched her eat bite after bite of strawberry pie. I finally got upset and said something like, "Hey, save a piece for me!" She liked to taunt me back then, and, as I recall, she continued to eat and withheld the pie from my grasp. Even being older, larger, and stronger than she was, I had to pry the pie away to salvage a piece for myself.

I was frustrated at not being permitted a piece of pie upon my first request, but grateful to have spared a piece of delicious pie for myself in the end. Kristin went upstairs to do homework or something lame—so I thought. It didn't seem like much longer from that point that my family's whole world came crashing down upon us.

I remember I finished eating the pie, and moments later, heard Kristin screaming, "Help me!" My mom ran up the stairs to learn that Kristin had taken some baking soda in order to make herself throw up.

Only once earlier do I recall learning that Kristin was struggling with an eating disorder. It was as we discussed the possibility of someone actually dying, like Karen Carpenter, a well-known musician.

Of course, being close in age to Kristin, I believe we fought like cats and dogs since we were babies and always bugged each other. My opinion may not have mattered to her, but I thought she was a cute and very outgoing girl. She did not need to do such things—as no one should—but I am sure my advice, especially since we did not traditionally get along, meant little. If I had only respected her earlier in life, our relationship could have been better. I now remember that, when we were younger, I even teased her about being heavy, and I have felt guilty; it is a shame that it took her death for me to feel this kind of guilt. Since her death, I have dealt with this guilt and believe I have forgiven myself to some degree.

American society is so absorbed with body image and disdain for those who are not "fit" or don't appear to be "healthy." Unfortunately, I believe that is why all the therapy in the world cannot cure us; only the therapy of true, unconditional love and acceptance for who and what we are can cure us.

I felt horribly guilty the year following Kristin's death due to us not always getting along and the comments I had made about her looking heavy when we were young. How I longed to tell her how beautiful and fun loving she was and wished I had the same relationship she had with her friends.

My belief in God and a life hereafter has given me peace in dealing with my sister's death.

I am living in Heber City, Utah, have four beautiful daughters and no boys (except a dog and guinea pig), and have been married almost twenty years. I have told my sister's story many times over the years and have felt that it helps me heal by telling the story. And though I'm not sure how it has helped others, I always hope it assures people that they are worth so much more than what they perhaps think they are personally worth. It has certainly helped me enjoy and appreciate people and life much more.

NICKY HAROLDSEN'S STORY

As I started thinking about this project, I began to realize that this is not Kristin's story—Kristin is not here to tell her story. This is Deborah's story and Rosemary's story and my dad's story and my story, and those stories share the role Kristin played in all of our different stories and the many lives she touched.

My story is from the perspective of the little sister who practically worshipped the ground Kristin walked on. Kristin meant the world to me; I always looked up to her as a very important role model in my life and would do anything for her. As a young child, I would sleep on the floor of her bedroom almost every night and loved that she wanted me to. Kristin was so much fun to be around and always had lots of friends and boyfriends. Her smile, sense of humor, and love of adventure—and mischief—were truly infectious. I was comparably shy by nature, but I aspired to be more like her and relished any attention she gave me.

I don't know at what point I became aware that she had an eating disorder, and I don't know if I even knew the term *bulimia*. As a twelve-year-old, I certainly did not know how dangerous it could be; however, I do recall her near obsession with the way she looked and that she would refer to herself as fat. I couldn't figure out why, because to me, she was perfect. But if she thought she was fat, I thought I must certainly be fat, too. We are all so critical of any of our perceived imperfections, no matter how minor. I know I was at least somewhat aware that she would make herself throw up, and it seems like whenever anyone would confront her about it, she would promise to stop. But self-perception is a powerful beast, and it got the better of her.

I was home the evening of May 1, 1986, and many of the events are still so vivid in my memory that it could've been yesterday. It was a perfectly normal spring evening; my brother David was out mowing the lawn after dinner in the warmth of the waning afternoon sun, my mom was on the phone, and I think I was watching TV. Kristin went upstairs to finish her homework so we could all watch *The Cosby Show* later. That's when the screams of agony began and my brother Mark started calling for Mom. She ended her phone call, and I followed her upstairs to see what was going on.

I watched from the background as my mom tried to stop Kristin from sticking her finger down her throat in an effort to throw up the baking soda that was causing her such pain. "I got to get it out, I got to get it out!" she kept saying in obvious distress. My mom helped her down the stairs and out to the car to take her to the hospital. I had no idea that would be the last time I would ever see my sister alive again.

The rest of the night is not nearly as clear in my memory. We went to my dad's house and waited nervously for any news. The next clear picture I have in my mind is of the following morning when I was in the bathroom getting ready for school, hoping it would be just another normal day and trying to ignore the knot in the pit of my stomach. I will never forget when my dad came into the room, took me by the shoulders, looked me in the eyes and said, "I don't think your sister's going to make it." Then he hugged me and we cried and cried. I don't think I stopped crying for a week. I definitely couldn't go to school. Could this really be happening? Was my sister really going to die?

Again, my memory gets a little fuzzy. My dad must have gone back to the hospital, and I waited at the house for my Aunt June and Uncle Lee to pick me up and take me there a little later. I remember the hospital lobby filling up with Kristin's friends—so many high school kids, flowers, and balloons. I think I was still in the elevator with my aunt and uncle when I heard the news that she was gone. What was I going to do without my big sister? I felt so hollow and alone and totally gypped. She was supposed to be there for me! I don't think I was angry with her; I was just angry, but I was mostly sad that she was gone.

I was twelve years old, right on the brink of puberty. I needed my big sister to help me through those challenging times of adolescence and all the struggles of growing up. Who was going to give me advice about boys or clothes or makeup? I felt like I didn't have anyone to turn to. I don't know if Deborah or Michelle or some of Kristin's other friends know how much it meant to me when they took me under their wings and made me feel like I almost had a big sister again.

In the next few years (decades?), I faced my own body image issues. As I got older, my body changed, and I gained weight—a story so familiar to young teenage girls and boys alike. By the time I was fourteen, I had outgrown all of Kristin's clothes (from when she was sixteen) that I had inherited. I felt fat, and I didn't know what to do about it. I knew what not to do; I knew that bulimia and anorexia could kill a person and that I would never dream of going down that path. But I didn't know how to lose weight in a healthy way either.

At that time, my mom was going around speaking to groups of young people about body image and the dangers of eating disorders. I was supposed to be OK with the way I was. If my mom asked me, I would tell her I was fine with the way my body looked, but I wasn't. All my friends were thinner than I was. My younger sister, Cammy, was thin, and even my stepmother was thin. It's hard not to compare yourself to others. I was never athletic, and our culture seems to practically teach us to hate exercise. I also knew that too much exercise could be dangerous as well. So I just internalized my insecurities and continued to gain weight. I was only a little overweight, but self-image is not always the same as reality, and how we feel can be stronger than what we are told.

I continued to struggle, and my weight fluctuated all through high school and college until somehow I finally found a balance between healthy eating habits, healthy exercise habits, and, most importantly and perhaps most difficultly, a healthy self-acceptance. Self-acceptance can't be taught and takes a lifetime of practice. I still place too much importance on my own physical appearance, and if I gain weight, I can get down on myself until I lose it again. But I am more forgiving of myself than ever as I continue to work toward unconditional love.

The first days, weeks, and about a year after Kristin's death were probably the hardest. Her absence was palpable and was on everyone's mind. I think that just going through normal day-to-day actions helped to get me through some tough times. Spending time with friends was also very important, even though we didn't talk much specifically about Kristin or her death. I remember asking my friend, Kristina, to get out of school and come over just to be with me.

My family and I have a solid Christian foundation, which has helped me; my belief in an afterlife especially gave some comfort in the months and years following Kristin's death. I still find comfort in the thought of Kristin as a kind of guardian angel in my life. I certainly hope to see her again someday.

I hope that if anything positive has come from our collective experience of losing our dear sister, friend, or daughter, it has been and will continue to be to raise awareness about this potentially deadly disorder and, in turn, help others overcome the challenges of body image and health.

Kristin is never far from my heart or my thoughts, and since her death, I have always thought of her as my guardian angel. I hope that she would be proud of the woman I have become. Each of our stories has continued since Kristin left them, but the impact she made on them in her short life will continue to affect us forever. I truly hope that in telling all of our stories we can positively change the outcome of the story of someone out there who might be suffering from some of these same issues. May we all strive for unconditional love of self.

DAVID HAROLDSEN'S STORY

"Kristin, you have to stop," I said, referring to her bulimia.

"I know I'm going to die," she said in a very lighthearted way, and then sort of skipped off down the hallway of our house. I don't think she really thought that was going to happen, and I didn't think that, but it was certainly strange that she said those words days before she actually died.

When it was all first happening, just before my mom rushed her to the hospital, I was spared seeing her suffer. I was in the backyard, oblivious, mowing the lawn, with no chance of hearing what was going on inside the house. When I finished and came inside, it was quiet because no one was there. I think I sort of wondered where everyone was, but didn't think much of it. It wasn't until later when she was at the hospital that I started to learn what was happening.

What I can remember next is being at my dad's house when he told me she was probably not going to make it. That is a very strange thing for a fourteen-year-old to hear, but it didn't hit me in the way you sort of imagine losing a sibling would. Yes, I was very sad, especially right when we all learned she was gone, being around everyone crying at the hospital, and I did cry there a lot, too, but I was also (after a day or two) maybe a little numb and wondered why I didn't feel worse (and felt a bit guilty about that).

I remember thinking that I would be getting a lot of attention from people at school and from my friends. But what happened was that people, especially my age, acted very strange and awkward around me (understandably), and even though I wanted attention and sympathy, after a while I realized I didn't really want to be treated much differently. I think this was one of the reasons my friends and I decided to sneak out in the middle of the night and "do something." We were thinking of Kristin and what we could do. I don't know whose idea it actually was, but we decided to do some spray painting.

For years there was a rectangular, vertical slab of asphalt up by the old mill that was ideal for painting messages, which people did regularly (there was layer after layer of paint). So we went up there in the middle of the night, and painted in big letters, "We'll miss you, Kris!" We would have written "Kristin," but, of course, we ran out of room. It was a small gesture, but lots of people saw it, and I'm really glad we did it. We had a picture of it on the side of our fridge for years after that.

Kristin was a wonderful big sister, and I loved her very much. She was always so great to me, and I felt a close connection to her. I have definitely missed Kris throughout my life. It is strange, though, that I can't really see my life being different than it was, so I don't spend much time thinking "what if." I'm just happy to have had her in my life for the first fourteen years during which she became a big part of me, as she did with so many others, and so she lives on.

In the year after Kristin's death, life more or less returned to normal. I remember going back to school at the junior high, and at that age, most people aren't yet skilled at showing empathy, and so with the exception of one friend (aside from my close friends who where around during the ordeal) reaching out with kind words, most of the kids around just acted as if nothing had happened. It felt odd at first, but for a lot of these people that I didn't know well, nothing really did happen, and for those that knew, I wouldn't expect a lot at that age, so it's really OK.

I got through the ordeal just by going on and living life, and it was OK. There was grieving and that is a good thing. Overall I believe that things happen and we can either accept them and grow from them or resist what is and suffer.

Kristin's death has helped me to live life more fully and know that life can be gone in an instant, so take nothing for granted.

CAMMY HAROLDSEN'S STORY

I was ten years old when Kristin went into the hospital that night and died the next morning. With six years between us, we pretty much did our own things and weren't especially close. Of course, I looked up to her and I know she watched out for me. I've often wondered how she would have influenced me and what our relationship would be like had she lived. What is apparent to me, however, is how profoundly what happened did influence me.

The night she went into the hospital, I was working out at a gym with friends. It was all very surreal to me. When I went to the hospital that morning, after hearing from my stepmom that Kristin probably wasn't going to make it, I had no real idea of what that would mean for my family, especially for my parents. I remember I wanted to be with my friends and that it was the only time I had seen my brother David cry.

After the shroud of mourning began to lift, my mom started investigating eating disorders and questioning our society's role in body image. She began to voice her criticisms of the media's objectification of women's bodies and how damaging it is to girls and women. As I went through adolescence, *diet* became a bad word in our house, and the phrase "eat when you're hungry; stop when you're full" was like a mantra. Sometimes I would get tired of hearing my mom's critique and analysis of what we saw on TV and in magazines, and I just wanted to watch TV without her commentary. But I became acutely aware that the big message out there really was "Be skinny!" My mom, in response, would say, "There are parts of a woman's body that are supposed to jiggle!"

I learned to recognize the damaging messages and began to forge a relationship with my body that was based on health and respect. The wonderfully supportive idea of what is important is who you are on the inside and not what you look like on the outside became, and continues to be, a foundational value for me.

I went with my mom when she talked to young women's groups about body image and eating disorders. I was moved by her fortitude to tell

Kristin's story over and over. Even though I was still a kid, I think I understood that my mom was telling this story in an effort to understand what happened, move through it, and, hopefully, save as many girls and women as she could from something so harmful.

Sometimes I wonder if any women in our society don't struggle with body image on some level. I feel like what happened to Kristin and my mom's response saved *me* from a life of fighting and disliking my body. Growing up, my friends knew this story and would think twice about how they talked about their bodies, and we'd remind ourselves that what is important is who we are, not what we look like.

From the age of ten on, the harmful messages about body image were replaced with ones of acceptance, compassion, health, and love. That's what Kristin and my mom have done for me, and it has affected every day of my life. My gratitude for them is endless.

Good *did* come of it. We all grew and got closer as a family. It heightened everyone's awareness about eating disorders and made us more conscientious of how what is important.

I've told her story dozens of times and have had many brief, but gentle, subtle connections with people through it by sharing stories and compassion.

After she died and since I was ten years old, I felt like Kristin was a guardian angel looking out for me. I am now thirty-eight. I do believe I am inextricably influenced and more sensitive to how people view and treat their bodies by *how* Kristin's died. I don't doubt, even for a second, that the body is any more important than our divine spirits that move us.

———

We can each go through the same thing yet experience it in such a different way depending on our relationship with a person or our age at the time. Going through something like losing a sibling is hard. I lost my youngest brother when he was twenty-six. You don't know what to feel. It took me so long to snap out of the funk that I was feeling. You feel numb.

Somehow you don't have to lose a person to death to experience the same feelings. You can feel the same way when your life is impacted by the actions of another person. If you aren't in control of what is happening, you feel helpless, and still the experience is impacting your entire life.

I encourage readers who are struggling with eating disorders to talk to others about what you are experiencing. For Kris's siblings, several of them never talked about what happened. For a couple of them, it wasn't until they were asked to put their feelings down on paper for this book that they had to stop and feel exactly what they experienced. Talking to others helps. Talk to someone that has experienced the same thing you are going through. Maybe you can get through it together. If you are the one going through a challenge like Kristin's that is impacting others, don't be blinded into believing that it is only affecting you—it's not.

I as well as many others were impacted by Kris's death. Kris thought that her decision to throw up to lose a few pounds would only affect her. She was wrong. I was by her side through the whole, long struggle, and it has affected me deeply.

CHAPTER 6

moving forward with hope

HOW DO YOU MOVE FORWARD?

After Kris's death, I felt such a void. I was in a fog, and it became hard to even get out of bed to go to school. I didn't know how to go on without her. How was I going to return to the high school knowing she wouldn't be there or knowing I wouldn't see her at our lockers to get a ride home? Why did she have to leave so young? Why did she have to leave me?

Kris died in May and school came to an end soon after that. My parents were worried about me, and they just wanted me to be happy, but I think they weren't sure what to do. I was sleeping a lot and wasn't interested in much. They didn't ask me how I was feeling. We didn't talk a lot about Kris's death; however, I knew that they cared through their actions towards me. My mom would leave me notes telling me that she loved me. They just didn't know what to say. Looking back now, I think that it would have been helpful for someone to talk to me and help me deal with her death, but instead I just put those feelings deep down inside and moved forward.

My mom's friend Marge called her and told her that her daughter was going away for the summer to be a nanny in New Jersey and asked if I wanted to go. My mom thought it would be good for me to get away from everything before we would have to go back to school again to start my junior year. After talking to my mom and dad about it, I agreed to be a nanny in New Jersey. The family I went to nanny for was great to me, and it turned out to be a wonderful experience. I was glad that I made the decision to go.

I did have reservations about coming home. I didn't know what to expect. My mom asked all of my friends to come to the airport to greet me, which they did. It was great to see them again. I hadn't realized how much I had missed them until we were reunited. I remember looking around for Kris, knowing she wouldn't be there but in a way hoping she would be. Each day after returning home things got a little easier. To be honest, it was really hard, but I seemed to get through one day at a time.

School started back up and life went on. It was hard for all of us: all of her friends, the Kids of America, and so many others missed her. Eating disorders were talked about a lot more often, and it was because of Kris that people were willing to speak up and start the conversation. Girls that had problems were willing to come forward and get help.

———————————

I still miss Kris even after almost three decades, and wish that she were here by my side, but she's not; however, even though she's not here, her story continues to help a lot of girls realize how serious an eating disorder can be, and it is because of Kris that many girls are still here today and are getting help.

I am a mother now and have three daughters; two of them are teenagers, and they are the same age that Kris and I were when she died. All of these years later, nothing has changed as far as needing to feel accepted and feeling that need to change yourself to be something that you're not. My daughter Hannah Kristin is a senior in high school and has shared with me stories of girls she goes to school with who have eating disorders. She asks me if she should speak up and tell someone. I tell her she absolutely should speak up and talk to the girls who are struggling.

My daughter Kenya is a sophomore in high school. She would tell you that body image problems are prominent, especially in sports. Girls are constantly looking in the mirror saying they look fat, and at lunch they talk about needing to start eating healthy and how they should count calories. She wants to tell those girls that we are all different; we just need to be confident in who we are. Girls of every age struggle with some type of body image problem and feel that no matter what they look like, it is not good enough.

Kris and I at times felt the need to change ourselves to be something different so that we would be accepted by others. I believe that some of those decisions contributed to Kris not feeling good enough in the way that she looked, and then in turn they contributed to Kris's eating disorder.

Instead of feeling the way Kris did, we must learn to feel comfortable thinking that this is who we are and that others should love us just the way we are. We shouldn't have to change.

How do you teach this? How do you teach people to love themselves? Can you teach people that they are perfect just the way they are? Why are we never content? Do we realize that our biggest cheerleaders are our family and friends around us? Yet those are the people we are the meanest to. At times we may feel alone. I know Kris did; if only she knew how many people really loved her and still love her.

I have a good friend whose daughter Amanda went off to college in the spring of 2011. Amanda had been struggling with an eating disorder. It all started a few years after she graduated from high school and went off to college to play soccer on a scholarship. She had worked her entire life to be a great soccer player, and she really enjoyed it. She had made good friends, and soccer truly made her happy. Soccer was one of the biggest parts of her life, right up to her final season. She was sad to see her soccer career end but tried to start focusing on school. It became hard; so much of who she was had been based on soccer. She started realizing how depressed she was and didn't know what to do with all of her free time. Soccer had defined her, and without it she was wondering what she was going to do.

She went about the normal college routine, but because of the depression she would forget to eat. People started noticing that she was losing weight and looking thin. They would mention to her how skinny she was looking, and she took it as a compliment that people were paying attention to her. As she lost more weight, she started enjoying it. It became an addiction. Things started getting worse, and her family realized that they needed to step in and get her help, which they did. She was able to get on some medication for the depression, but she couldn't stop the eating disorder. They had her move home, but things continued to get worse. There were other siblings in the home and she consumed all of her parents' time, which caused major problems.

Early on I was able to share Kris's story with her. I told her what it was like to be by her side through her ups and downs. I told her how much I love Kris, and I know Kris would have loved her. I wanted Amanda to know that a lot of people were cheering her on and hoping she can fight this addiction. She didn't have to have the same ending as Kris; she could overcome and beat this.

She has started to heal since that time. I have watched her throughout the process, and I recently had the chance to sit down with her to see how she was doing. I talked to Amanda about how she is moving forward and healing the damage of the addiction. She gave me wonderful advice and insights that I wanted to share.

AMANDA'S STORY

As I look back at photos when I was at college and really struggling with the eating disorder, I see that I was really thin, but I liked it. People now ask me, "How are you doing with your eating disorder now?" I tell them, "I am healthy today, but every day is a struggle." I don't think people realize it isn't something that you just get over—it is a struggle every single day. When I think about when I was my thinnest and I think I look good, I am reminded that those were also some of my saddest and darkest days, and I don't want to go back there.

To those who struggle with an eating disorder today, my story is one of hope. I want you to know that it can get better, but you are going to have to try your hardest, and it isn't going to come easy. Do what you *have* to do for yourself. It may be the hardest now, but it will be the best in the end. Love yourself. Listen to people who are trying to help you. You have to accept that people want to help you, especially your family.

———————————

Amanda is a beautiful girl in her early twenties. She has her entire life ahead of her and could accomplish anything, but for now she just takes life one day at a time. She realizes that she needs to stay on medication for her depression. She is now realizing that she can't do it on her own and it is OK.

I asked Amanda what advice she would give parents who have a child struggling with an eating disorder. She replied, "Just love them. No matter how hard it may be at times, just keep loving them. One thing my mom did for me that showed me that she loved me was when she cooked for our family and always made sure there was something for me to eat. If she was cooking steak and knew I didn't eat red meat, she would cook me chicken. That showed me love." Parents want to know everything and are sometimes overbearing. About this, Amanda said, "Let your child know that you are there for them, but don't try to pry and push; they will come to you when they are ready."

Although the story of Amanda is not yet over, she is alive and doing well. Amanda wants to help others just like I hope Kris's story will. Here are a few thoughts that Amanda wanted to share.

1. **Learn to love yourself.** Learning to love yourself is a process. It isn't something that magically happens overnight. Every experience we go through in this life comes with a lesson. It does one of two things: makes you a better person or does nothing for you. The purpose of this life is to progress and grow as people, and in order for that to happen we must experience opposition in all things. Without the feelings of sadness, we would never know the feelings of happiness. It is hard to teach people how to love themselves. When I hear the word *learn*, it sounds scary and overwhelming, but that is why we are here in this life. If we don't learn from our mistakes or experiences we will never grow and we will never reach our potential. Learning can be enjoyable if you let it. It really doesn't matter what other people think of you, but it matters what you think of yourself.

2. **If you aren't happy, change something.** It doesn't have to be a drastic change. Start changing the little things. Recognize what is

holding you back from being truly happy. It can be certain people or even something you are doing or aren't doing. Whatever it is, change it. It can be one of the hardest things, but nothing is better than the feeling of true happiness. It is worth it.

3. **I am in control.** I am the *only* person who decides my happiness. One of my favorite quotes says, "No one can make you feel inferior without your consent." I have heard that a million times, but I never fully understood it until I went through some of the darkest times in my life. I can choose to be miserable, or I can accept who I am and not be ashamed of it. At any given time I have the ability to change my course.

4. **It is okay to be a little bit selfish.** I find being selfish hard sometimes because we are often taught to be selfless and to think of others before ourselves. In my opinion, people can't help others reach higher ground if they themselves aren't settled on solid ground. I found that by setting goals and following through on them provided me with something to work toward and helped me feel the sense of accomplishment. Find a balance of helping yourself as well as thinking of others.

5. **Don't wait to be happy.** Accept what is happening and change what you can. Be happy *now*. Instead of thinking *I will be happy as soon as finals are over* or *I will be happy when I lose five pounds*, enjoy where you are now.

6. **Perfection will never be achieved in this lifetime.** Trying to please everyone and making him or her happy made me miserable. It was frustrating and exhausting. There were, and still are times that I get discouraged and feel as if I have failed, but I will never fail until I have quit trying.

7. **Don't take people for granted.** Through this experience I have lost some really good friends, but I have also gained some of the closest friends that are so dear to me.

8. **Remember the way you felt.** Write down your feelings in a journal. Find the times you were the happiest and see who was in your life and what it is you were doing. When were you the saddest? What was happening and what influenced you to feel this way? Remember

why you felt the way you did and why you do or do not want to feel that way again. Remember the past to teach you, but don't dwell there. Focus on the future.

9. **Find things that bring *you* happiness.** They can be simple or extreme, but find what you love to do! It's OK if you don't know. Discover what your talents, strengths, and weaknesses are. Once you have found them, use them. There are people in the world who need *you*. Explore your options. Try things you have never done before or go back to doing the things that once made you happy and see if they still bring the happiness you once felt. Don't be discouraged if they don't bring back the feeling you once had. There are so many options out there, and nothing is set in stone. It is never too late to change or to try something new.

10. ***Do not* compare yourself to others.** There are no two people in this world who are exactly the same, and there is a reason for that. We were all born with various talents, and we were given them to help the people who come into our lives. Everyone has a story.

11. **Surround yourself with people who uplift you.** This might sound cliché, but it can be one of the hardest things you will ever have to do and can completely change your life. It's easy to be around certain people because of habit. You might not realize the negative impact they have on you because that's all you're used to. Don't push away the people who love you and want to help. They aren't doing it to hurt you. They do what they do because they love you. It's ironic that we hurt the people who love us the most.

12. **Train your mind to have positive thoughts.** You believe what you tell yourself. Positive thoughts and words will bring a positive life. It is impossible to be negative if you give yourself positive feedback. It is impossible to be happy and positive if you are giving yourself negative feedback. You attract positive people and are able to uplift others by being positive yourself.

13. **Remember, it does get better.** I hated more than anything when people would tell me this. Of course they could say that because they weren't feeling what I was feeling. But they were right. People may come and go and difficult situations arise, but it passes and there are

always better days. Have hope and faith that they will. If you've hit rock bottom, you truly can only go up from there, but *you* have to decide.

There isn't a day that goes by that I don't have thoughts along the lines of, "I should stop eating to lose weight," "I should count my calories," "Only 1,200 calories a day," or "I'll just eat whatever I want and then throw it all up." What prevents me from falling back into that dark hole I was once in is remembering the feelings of sadness, misery, unhappiness, anger, frustration, and disappointment that I came across. I remember the feelings I had when I realized I was hurting the ones I loved as well as the ones who loved me.

It is a constant battle, but I am proud to look back and see how far I have come. It shows me that soccer isn't the only thing in life that I can succeed in or that makes me feel accomplished. I learned to accomplish what I wanted in soccer through hard work, dedication, practice, and effort. This has taught me that I can accomplish whatever I set my mind to.

I am currently going to school at a university, and I will be taking the next semester off to work full time. I have found that keeping myself busy with things that I enjoy and people that I love keeps me happy. I have built some of my greatest friendships through this experience. I have figured out who my true friends are and who I can trust. I have found that my family will always love me unconditionally, and I will always love them. They want only the best for me and do only what is in my best interest.

––––––––––––––

After sitting down with Amanda, I am grateful to her for being willing to share her ups and downs with me and for sharing her story. I realize the pain she has had to endure and will continue to endure. Parents sometimes want a quick fix: snap out of it, get over it. But it isn't going to happen, and parents just need to love and accept the way it is, just like Amanda said. Parents need to constantly remind their children, starting when they're at a very young age, how beautiful (on the inside and out) they are and how wonderful they are.

And this isn't limited to our daughters. In addition to the two teenage daughters I mentioned before, I also have another girl and six boys. My boys have the same need to learn to love themselves unconditionally. Boys struggle with being too thin or too short for sports, and they also want to be something different than they are.

The education for all children starts with parents. Children mirror what their parents say, and they need and want to hear compliments from their parents. Children need to be constantly reminded, starting at a very young age, how wonderful and beautiful (on the inside and out) they are and that their parents believe in them. Believing in your child is one of the greatest gifts parents can give to them.

Ten years after Kris died, I went to bed and for the first time since her death, I dreamt about her. I had always thought about her during those years, but this was the first dream I had about her. This dream was different than anything I had ever experienced before. At that time of the dream my family was living in a sixplex; there were three apartments upstairs and three downstairs. When we opened our front door we would walk out of our apartment and down eight steps onto the asphalt where we would park our cars.

In the dream, I was in the front room of our apartment playing with my two toddlers that I had at the time. A knock came at my front door. I opened the door and there stood Kris—not at the age of sixteen as I remembered her, but at the same age that I was at the time of the dream. She had long blonde hair and a big smile on her face. I immediately gave her a hug and asked her to come in. We sat on my couch for hours and talked. We caught up with life and everything that had happened since she had died. She told me she was happy and that she was OK. We picked up right where we had left off, after the day when she dropped me off at my house and said, "Love ya, kid."

I didn't want to say goodbye, but I remember her standing up and motioning toward the front door. I told her I loved her. She said to me, "Tell my mom I love her and that I am OK." I opened the front door and hugged her one last time. She walked down the steps and was gone. Gone from my dreams and gone from my life once again, but I felt happy.

I woke up and felt as if I were never asleep. I wrote all of it down in my journal. I never did dream about her again after that, but I finally had closure. I can't explain what had happened or how I was feeling, but for the first time in a long time I knew that Kris was OK and that everything was going to be alright.

There isn't a day that goes by for me that Kris isn't by my side—in my thoughts and in my heart. I wonder what things would have been like today. I would still be getting together with her from time to time to discuss our kids and lives. She would have been a wonderful mother. I know she would want to tell each of us to be happy with ourselves, find happiness, and accept who we are.

If you know someone with an eating disorder, speak up and let them know that you care about them. Let them know that they are loved and that they are beautiful.

To you who are struggling with an eating disorder, remember: You can move forward, and there is hope. Just look around you at all the people who care about you and who are cheering you on.

You are beautiful, and I believe in you.

PART 2

Eating Disorders

CHAPTER SEVEN

eating disorders 101

In reading the accounts of close family members and friends, it's easy to see that there were many important relationships in Kristin's life. Time and time again, the people in Kristin's life describe Kristin as being loveable, kind, fun to be around, and beautiful from the inside out. There were many people in her life that cared a great deal about her. Sadly, one of her most significant relationships was kept a secret—her relationship with "Ed" (a personification of eating disorders). She kept quiet her thoughts and hid her behaviors in order to protect Ed and hide it from the family members and friends who cared so deeply about her. Unfortunately, when they were made aware of the seriousness of her relationship with Ed, it was too late.

Eating disorders are very complex illnesses that develop over time. While invdividuals may initially choose to engage in compulsive behaviors related to eating disorders, they do not choose the illness that it progresses into. Just as someone who drinks their first alcoholic beverage has no intention of becoming an alcoholic and doesn't see in that moment that what they are doing could potentially lead to the disease of alcoholism. As a result, there is no pure understanding of where eating disorders come from, just as there is no way to know for sure who will and who won't become an alcoholic.

What we do know about is causation and the risk factors that make someone more likely to develop an eating disorder. Some of this has to do with genetics and the way our bodies respond to the biological changes created by stress and distress in our lives. Individuals are more susceptible to developing an eating disorder if any of the following risk factors are present:

- Family members with eating disorders
- Family history of depression
- Family history of anxiety
- High BMI (body mass index) during sexual development (approximately ages 9–12)
- Early onset of menstrual cycle
- Personality temperament (perfectionism, constant worrying, impulsivity, harm avoidant)
- History of extreme and frequent dieting
- Exposure to the fashion industry
- Participation in activities where body type is linked to performance (dancers, swimmers, cheerleaders, jockeys, etc.)

It is not the purpose of this book to explore the specific etiology and development of this illness; however, the purpose is to convey basic information in an effort to raise awareness and provide education of this deadly illness. There are many different views regarding eating disorders and the way in which they need to be treated. The specific way in which professionals view the illness serves as the basis for treatment approaches. For example, if the eating disorder is viewed as a medical illness, then the treatment approach might focus on nourishing the brain in order to heal the individual.

One way of viewing eating disorders is as an addiction. As mentioned previously, individuals may choose to initially engage in behaviors. Over time and with repeated instances, their compulsive behaviors can progress into a full-blown eating disorder—or addiction. The undertone of this book suggests that eating disorders are a form of addiction. In many ways, eating disorders are very similar to other addictions. For individuals with an eating disorder, it serves an immediate purpose and offers comfort for them during their most difficult and desperate hours. As with other addictions, eating disorders can become the negative, go-to coping skills as well as self-destructive behaviors that suffering people utilize to help them manage life.

For the past ten years, I have had the opportunity to work in a residential treatment center for women struggling with eating disorders and other addictions. It has been an amazing and life-changing experience to help these beautiful women along their very difficult journey to recovery. I wholeheartedly believe that people can learn, grow, and make changes in their lives. People can get well and be set free from the grasps of addiction if they choose to.

There is much to be learned and valuable insight to gain from reading Kristin's story. Hers was a story of how easy it is to miss the warning signs and red flags of an eating disorder until, sadly, it is too late. There is also a lot to learn from stories of those who have been tangled in the turmoil of this illness and been fortunate enough to live to see a better, happier, and healthier life—a life freed from the eating disorder. Thankfully, not every story has to end as Kristin's did.

Our hope is to generate some basic awareness of this mental illness and to shed some light on the fact that there is hope. Healing can be found. And recovery is possible for those who genuinely want it.

UNDERSTANDING THE DISORDERS

Throughout the years, I have been asked by many people what I do for a living. I learned very early on that my response would generate a mixture of admiration, appreciation, questions, and great conversation. Whether I'm speaking with a man or a woman, of any age, just the mention of eating disorders seems to pique interest. As soon as I describe the population I work with, people want to know, in a nutshell, everything there is to know about eating disorders. People are curious and want to know more about the mysterious illness they rarely hear specific details about; however, if you ask people who have suffered from this illness or who have worked closely around it, they will tell you that there isn't a nutshell big enough to even begin to educate someone on the topic. It is far too complex and often times too confusing to simply fit into one short conversation.

Most people would say, "It's easy; they just need to eat." This way of thinking suggests that there is a lack of understanding, because eating disorders are about more than just needing to eat.

Along with the questions and conversations, my response also unintentionally provokes some very ignorant and uneducated comments. I'm always surprised by how many people (jokingly or not) will say to me, "I wish I had an eating disorder," or "I have one of those . . . I eat everything in sight." They laugh about their comments as if it's the first time anyone has ever said that to me and then carry on with their day. In their minds, they are equating an eating disorder to those extra ten pounds they want to lose or to having an extra piece of pie for dessert.

The truth is that eating disorders are so much more complicated than that. For people with eating disorders, it becomes a way of life, an obsession, an addiction, a compulsive process that controls their thoughts and behaviors day in and day out. It's as if they are constantly swimming in a sea of self-doubt, insecurities, shame, and guilt. If having an eating disorder sounds exhausting and a bit overwhelming, that's because it can be.

For the people inquiring about what I do, our conversation comes and goes. In reality, they have no idea what they are referring to and wishing for. I smile and end the conversation, all the while knowing the seriousness of the illness they are so misinformed about. It is easier to laugh with them—or sometimes at them—than it is to explain the severity of what they are so lightheartedly joking about.

People would never even consider making jokes about cancer or wish to be diagnosed with it. Nothing about that would be funny because there is awareness of the tragedy it can bring to so many people. The harsh realities of cancer are well known, often talked about, and prevalent in our society.

Unfortunately, the same widespread knowledge and understanding doesn't apply as much to eating disorders. And, for whatever reason, people feel comfortable to laugh and joke about the things they don't understand or don't know very much about. If people truly understood the severity of the impact that eating disorders have on the lives of those affected, they might be surprised to learn that eating disorders are certainly nothing to joke about. A review of nearly fifty years of research confirms that anorexia nervosa has the highest mortality rate of any psychiatric disorder. This is definitely not something to wish for! That's an alarming and unsettling statistic when you consider the vast array of mental illness present in our society today. We are in need of a population better informed and able to support those who struggle with this illness.

LOOKING INSIDE THE DISORDER

To give you a tiny glimpse into the mentality of an eating disorder, let us consider a scenario that could take place for anyone. I want you to imagine for a minute that you hear your phone ringing. You pick up your phone and see that one of your best friends is calling. You are very excited because this is a good friend whom you haven't been able to connect with in a while. You answer the phone call and begin the normal chitchat that most people do. You might talk about how you've been, what your family is up to, the latest trip you went on, or some other part of your day-to-day life. It's an easy conversation that you can only have with your closest friend. You know the kind of friend; you pick up right where you left off regardless of how much time has actually passed. It's as if you just talked on the phone yesterday.

However, as the conversation continues, you learn that your friend didn't only call to chitchat and catch up; your friend called to invite you to attend a work event. It's a night out for dinner at one of the greatest restaurants in town. And the best part is that the entire evening is going to be paid for by your friend's employer. Most people would welcome the invitation, graciously accept, and look forward to the event with excitement. Some might even consider going shopping to find a new outfit to wear for the occasion. However, people with an eating disorder might act as though they are happy to be invited, hesitantly accept the invitation, and hang up the phone only to experience shear dread and panic. This scenario sounds dramatic but sadly isn't too far from the truth. Once that indivudual hangs up the phone, it's highly likely that the eating disorder takes over and his or her mind begins to race. In the moments to follow, the conversation in his or her head might sound something like this:

How am I supposed to eat in front of people at a nice restaurant? What if everyone at the table listens to what I order and then watches me eat . . . or not eat? What if there is a buffet and I can't control myself? I would feel so bad wasting someone else's money on an expensive meal that I know I'm just going to throw up. I would hate to binge and purge at a fancy restaurant or have my friend find out what I'm doing. I don't have anything to wear that won't make me stand out and look fat. I would be so scared and so uncomfortable in that setting. There are way too many triggers for me around people and food. I just don't trust that I could act normal, I'm sure I can get out of going to it somehow.

This internal dialogue gives an idea as to how quickly the negative thoughts and self-defeating banter spirals out of control. Most likely, within minutes of hanging up the phone, he or she will have talked themselves right out of attending the event. Although he or she cares about their friend and their relationship, the thought of going out to eat with so many people can be too scary and too overwhelming. Making up an excuse in order to avoid it altogether might seem much easier. In that moment, he or she decides to call their friend at some point and cancel. Keep in mind that he or she has no intention of hurting the friend or neglecting the friendship, but the thought of actually going is too much to deal with. The eating disorder wins and he or she misses out.

When it comes to scenarios like this, all addictions have something in common. In the end, the people struggling are left all alone. My observation has been that it is very common for those struggling to withdraw and become isolated so that events, occasions, people, places, and relationships don't get in the way of them carrying out their negative behaviors and causing unwelcomed anxiety. They are completely loyal to their illness at the expense of abandoning relationships, lying to people that they care about, and feeling extremely sad, lonely, and depressed. They create their own little world that includes them and their "best friend"—the illness.

SEEING THE REALITY OF EATING DISORDERS

Think for a minute of the phrase *eating disorder* and pay attention to the images that pop up in your mind. I would be willing to bet that you picture a frail, young teenage girl whose bones are visible and whose cheeks are sunken in. Or maybe you envision a stick-thin fashion model wearing a flashy dress and strutting down a runway. If those are the images that automatically come into your head, you're not alone. Most people would see the same images or something very similar in their minds.

The problem with those images is that they play into the stereotypical idea of an eating disorder. The reality is that eating disorders come in all shapes and sizes. Not everyone affected by this illness looks like a stick-thin model or a frail little girl. In the United States, twenty million women and ten million men suffer from a clinically significant eating disorder at some time in their lives, including anorexia nervosa, bulimia nervosa, binge eating disorder, or other specified feeding or eating disorder (OSFED). Like other addictions, eating disorders (ED) don't discriminate.

I've often heard people of the baby boomer generation say, "Oh, those things weren't around when I was growing up; it's just a fad," or "Girls just do that to get attention." The truth is that eating disorders aren't just a fad and have been around for many, many years; however, it hasn't been until the past couple of decades that people paid enough attention to really talk about them and start to understand the underlying issues intertwined in the illness.

For many people, the death of Karen Carpenter, a famous singer and drummer during the 1970s, in 1983 brought to the forefront the idea of an eating disorder. As shocking as it may seem, it's very unlikely that she was the only one of her generation to suffer from this devastating illness. Her death certainly opened the door for awareness of eating disorders and generated conversations about their reality.

Since that time, there has been a lot of research and discussion on the topic. It is common to see brief stories about them in the news or on talk shows. Many mental health professionals believe that eating disorders are a learned behavior and that people develop them as a way to cope with negative life experiences. This belief would imply that humans aren't born with an innate sense to dislike food or hate their body. Rather, the illness is a result of environmental factors and life experiences that are too unbearable for some people to handle in healthy ways. Fortunately, this belief suggests that eating disorders can be unlearned and that there is hope for those trapped inside of the eating disorder mentality.

BECOMING AWARE OF EATING DISORDERS

As Kristin's story suggests, eating disorders are very complex, secretive, harmful, and destructive mental illnesses. Promoting education and raising awareness is a vital part of the battle we face against eating disorders because the illness is so complex, making it difficult to fully understand. There is great benefit in making an effort to understand them from many angles, including but not limited to genetic vulnerability, environmental factors (both physical and social), and mental and emotional stability. Not only is there power in knowledge, but there is also a chance that more lives can be saved if we know what to look for and how to help.

When we hear that someone has cancer, oftentimes the first question we think to ask them is what kind of cancer they have. Once we know, it's likely that we go to the computer, get on the Internet, and learn everything there is to know about the particular type of cancer. By knowing what type of cancer someone is battling, we can have an idea of what his or her treatment might look like or what his or her prognosis might be. As hard as it is to hear about a loved one or close friend who has been diagnosed with cancer, there is a little piece of comfort that comes with knowledge and understanding.

The same is true of illnesses like eating disorders. It is scary to learn that someone close to you is struggling with something so difficult, and oftentimes what makes it seem scary is a lack of understanding. This lack of knowledge can lead us to fear the worst possible outcome, and that is a very hopeless feeling. It's important and helpful to understand the different types of eating disorders as well as some of the reasons someone might engage in these behaviors.

In this chapter we will look at the different types of eating disorders in a simple, straightforward manner. We will explore some of the reasons why someone might develop an eating disorder in later chapters. Understanding some of the basic things about eating disorders can help us better comprehend the difficulties one might have in overcoming his or her battle as well as how we can help.

ANOREXIA NERVOSA

Most people have probably heard the term *anorexia* and have a vague understanding of what it means. Simply put, anorexia is self-starvation. People with anorexia will restrict their caloric intake to the point of starving their body of the nutrients needed. They avoid taking in food or limit their food intake for many days at a time in an effort to lose weight and become thinner. They may eat but often have very strict food rules that they have to follow. For example, they might only allow themselves to eat a particular food item, like lettuce, carrots, grilled chicken, cottage cheese, one cracker, and so on. The actual food item isn't what's important. The more important thing to pay attention to is that they even have certain, specific food rules that they have to follow each and every day.

If you know what to look for, some of the signs of anorexia are more obvious than others. Those suffering from eating disorders may become obsessed with being thin and begin counting every calorie in food items. Their obsession with calories and food may also lead them to collect recipes. It's common for those struggling with this illness to chew food and spit it out or to move food around on their plate to make it appear as if they have eaten more than they really have. They may also tear food items apart to make them appear smaller or to allow some of the calories to drop off as crumbs.

Those who struggle with anorexia suffer from insecurities and oftentimes will wear baggy clothes to hide their bodies. This also helps them to feel unnoticed because people can't see their shape or their curves.

On the other hand, if those with anorexia are very proud of their anorexic body (known as *anorexic pride*), they might wear very tight-fitting clothes to show off how little their bodies are. They might even buy clothes in kid or junior sizes even though they are adults—just because they can.

Individuals with anorexia are often high achievers, rigid, and strive for perfection. Although many are accomplished and successful, they feel less than and undeserving, and they feel like they've failed if they can't be perfect in every way. Anorexia embraces a very black and white way of viewing the world; there is very little gray. If there is any gray, it can be very difficult for them to see.

Many with anorexia also struggle with depression. This can make it difficult for professionals to determine if the depression is a result of the anorexia or vice versa. In either situation, many who seek treatment are prescribed medication to help with their depressive symptoms.

Anorexia poses some very serious health risks to the individual engaging in these behaviors, some of which are dehydration, low blood pressure, low heart rate, osteoporosis, iron deficiency, thinning and loss of hair, discoloration of skin, kidney dysfunction, heart problems, loss of teeth, and swollen glands. They may become very tired and very weak and lose a lot of their muscle functions. Obviously, the seriousness of the medical problems may increase the longer the body is deprived of nourishment.

Because those with anorexia are malnourished, they usually don't have enough body fat to stay warm. In an effort to stay warm, those with anorexia might develop what is known as *lanugo*. This is a condition in which a thin layer of hair grows on the body. Some refer to it as *peach fuzz*. The thin hair appears on the face first and then appears on other parts of the body. It is the body's natural way of keeping warm when so little body fat is present.

Another side effect of anorexia resulting from extremely low body fat is called *amenorrhea*. This is when a female stops menstruating because she has lost so much weight. The side effects previously mentioned are oftentimes negative consequences that someone with anorexia might experience; however, this side effect is perceived a little differently.

Most women would love to eliminate the dreaded monthly cycle, but women with anorexia are able to accomplish this and lose weight at the same time. In a woman's world, this is a win-win. Suffice it to say, this change in their body may become a measurement in their mind as to whether or not they are maintaining a low enough body weight. It can be very scary and upsetting to someone with anorexia if and when her menstrual cycle returns, as this would be an indication that her body weight and body fat have increased.

Those with anorexia may also learn later in life that they are infertile and have a very difficult time conceiving. Not only can this be upsetting for a woman with the desire to bear children, but it also plays into the cycle of shame, guilt, disappointment, and disgust she may already feel toward her body.

BULIMIA NERVOSA

As we learned from Kristin's story, another kind of eating disorder that people may struggle with is called bulimia nervosa. Bulimia is characterized by consuming large quantities of food and then eliminating it from the body through purging. This behavior is also known as a binge/purge cycle. People with bulimia might binge and purge once in a while or multiple times per day. They usually binge on high caloric or high carbohydrate foods. Some with bulimia may spend hours on end repeating this detrimental cycle to experience the rush that comes with purging and the false sense of control over and over again.

From time to time, we've all experienced that overwhelming full feeling after consuming a large meal. For most, it's probably associated with Thanksgiving dinner or the occasional celebration where there is a large array of food available. We might think in that moment that we would do just about anything to get rid of that overfull feeling. Well, that is exactly the feeling that individuals with bulimia desire—not so much the feeling of being full, but the rush they experience from getting rid of the excessive amounts of food consumed. This rush is very similar to the rush a drug addict experiences from taking a hit or smoking to get high.

As we clearly learned from Kristin's battle with an eating disorder, bulimia can have harmful and shocking outcomes. Many of the physical side effects of bulimia are hard to recognize until the illness is so far developed that it has already damaged the body from the inside out. Unlike people with anorexia, those with bulimia typically don't lose weight in the same extreme ways. The illness can go unnoticed because people with bulimia don't always appear to be as visibly thin as those suffering from anorexia. Take Kristin for example—a vivacious, young, attractive girl with a round face and an average, curvy body. Nothing about her appearance screamed eating disorder to those around her, and, sadly, she didn't receive the help she needed in time.

It's ironic that individuals with bulimia have a tendency to believe that binging and purging will help balance things out in their bodies, because the opposite is actually true. They believe that all they have to do after taking food in is to expel the food out in order to control the number on the scale; however, that ends up throwing off everything in their bodies.

Electrolyte imbalance is caused by dehydration and loss of potassium, sodium, and chloride from the body as a result of purging behaviors. Electrolyte imbalances can lead to irregular heartbeats and possibly heart failure and death. The act of purging also causes stomach acid to pass through the mouth. This can lead to tooth decay or even tooth loss. The esophagus may become inflamed or even rupture from the strain of excessive purging. This is extremely dangerous and life threatening for those with bulimia because they risk bleeding out before they are able to get help.

Many people who struggle with bulimia are in pursuit of acquiring control in their lives. The illness helps them gain a false sense of control when in reality their compulsive behaviors are out of control. They may feel as if they are "in control" of the calories they are absorbing and the number on the scale. People who suffer with bulimia become obsessed with food and the act of binging and purging. They obsess about the number on the scale and may even weigh themselves before eating, after eating, and after purging just to make sure that their behavior is being rewarded by a decreasing number on the scale. Just as a drug addict might have an immediate craving and need to get high, those with bulimia may have an immediate need and craving to feel the rush from binging and purging food.

They may also try to restrict their food intake as those with anorexia do, but this leaves them thinking about and craving food until the compulsion to binge takes over. There is a lot of shame, guilt, and embarrassment that follows binging episodes. These can be some of the feelings that contribute to their low self-esteem. Their solution to counteract what they have done is to purge the food and get rid of the calories. One potential sign that someone may be suffering from bulimia is if he or she makes frequent trips to the bathroom immediately after eating. Other behaviors that accompany bulimia are dishonesty and secrecy. Hoarding or even stealing food is common for people who suffer from this illness.

OTHER DISORDERS

Anorexia and bulimia are the most well-known types of eating disorders, but there are other categories of eating disorders that are worth mentioning as well. Individuals who struggle with this illness don't always fit into one category or the other. Their behaviors might include pieces of each disorder. For example, someone might be referred to as having *anorexia-binge/purge type*. This means that they meet many of the diagnostic criteria for anorexia, including extremely low body weight, but they also engage in binging and purging as someone with bulimia would. It's not uncommon for someone with anorexia to go through episodes during which he or she engages in bulimic behaviors. Similarly, many with bulimia have been known to become anorexic as their decrease in body weight becomes more and more appealing over time.

Another disorder is binge eating disorder (BED). This disorder is when a person engages in uncontrolled eating behaviors. Oftentimes the episodes are frequent and very impulsive. A person with BED will consume food until or even past the point of discomfort. Those who struggle with BED are often obese and at a higher risk for cardiovascular disease and high blood pressure.

People with BED indulge in what is known as *emotional eating.* This is when people binge on food in an effort to feel comforted or to try and fill a void in their lives. They turn to food instead of utilizing healthy coping skills to address their emotional difficulties. People struggling with binge eating disorder are likely managing their emotions through food.

As mentioned in the beginning of the chapter, there is another category of eating disorder called *other specified feeding or eating disorder* (OSFED). This is actually the diagnosis most people with eating disorders fall into. It is possible for someone to have many of the characteristics and behaviors of anorexia or bulimia without meeting all of the criteria to be diagnosed with one or the other. For example, people might engage in overexercising to purge calories instead of actually vomiting the food they have eaten. They may have disordered eating habits and food rules that they have to strictly follow in order to be in control of their lives and their weight.

OSFED recognizes that there are eating disorder behaviors from one end of the spectrum to the other and that people may engage in some but not all of them. Comments posted to the *Jenni Schaefer Blog* on August 21, 2013, describe this diagnosis with five subtypes including:

1. Atypical Anorexia Nervosa (i.e., anorexic features without low weight)
2. Bulimia Nervosa (of low frequency and/or limited duration)
3. Binge Eating Disorder (of low frequency and/or limited duration)
4. Purging Disorder
5. Night Eating Syndrome

The Diagnostic and Statistical Manual of Mental Disorders (DSM-5) also includes a category called Unspecified Feeding or Eating Disorder (UFED) that is reserved for those who don't fit into any of these five categories, or for whom there is not enough information to make a specific OSFED diagnosis.

UNDERSTANDING WHY

You may read this and think it seems insignificant for people to want to overexercise in an effort to get rid of unwanted calories or to be health conscious in the choices they make in their diet. But there is a fine line between participating in enjoyable exercise for health reasons and having to exercise to make sure you are working off all of the calories you have eaten in a day or more. Likewise, there is nothing wrong with wanting to make healthy food choices. However, it is a problem when the food choices dictate your life and you have food rules you have to follow or else you will feel extreme guilt and shame. Similar to compulsive processes and addictions, the obsessive thoughts, triggers, and behaviors have to start somewhere.

References

Arcelus, Jon, Alex Mitchell, Jackie Wales, & Søren Nielsen. "Mortality Rates in Patients with Anorexia Nervosa and Other Eating Disorders." *Archives of General Psychiatry*, 68, no. 7 (2011):724–731.

National Eating Disorders Association (NEDA). Accessed May 30, 2014. www.nationaleatingdisorders.org.

Wade, Tracy. D., Ana Keski-Rahkonen, and James Hudson. "Epidemiology of Eating Disorders." In *Textbook of Psychiatric Epidemiology*, edited by Ming Tsuang, Mauricio Tohen, and Peter Jones, 343–60. New York: Wiley, 2011.

CHAPTER EIGHT

some reasons why

To attempt to answer the question as to why someone would engage in eating disorder behaviors or develop an eating disorder can be complicated. It's important to remember that there are many things that can be found at the core of the illness, such as genetic vulnerability, low self-esteem, feelings of worthlessness, or negative body image, to name a few. Over time, the compulsive behaviors can become more frequent and present in a way that looks like addiction.

The very nature of an addiction suggests a compulsive need for a habit-forming substance or behavior and use of that substance or behavior. It's very unlikely that people set a goal to become addicted to these destructive habits. Unfortunately, over time and with repeated instances, the compulsive behaviors can develop into addiction and take hold physically, mentally, emotionally, and spiritually. The whole person is affected by the illness.

I've often heard those addicted to substances say, "I didn't intend to become an addict. I just wanted to use it once to see what it was like, but then I couldn't stop." Some people are prewired and predisposed to have addictive behaviors and tendencies. In the case of people who "just wanted to try it" and then couldn't stop, it's very possible that they have a history of addiction in their family, as if there is an addictive gene that gets passed down from generation to generation. As a result, they are genetically vulnerable and at a higher risk to develop addictions.

The concept of being predisposed to addictive behaviors can apply to eating disorders as well. There are many people who suffer from the illness who never intended to have an eating disorder. Their intention may have started as a diet to lose a little extra weight or a New Year's resolution to eat healthier and exercise more. Changes like this need to be monitored and kept in check so they don't become unhealthy. Otherwise, their intentions may progress into compulsive behaviors that can very easily develop into a more destructive mindset resulting in addiction.

Surely, addictions of all kinds can be the result of innocent actions and behaviors that have gone too far. People may want to use drugs in a recreational way and later become addicted and spiral out of control. It is possible for the diet mentality to get out of control, become obsessive, and lead to disordered eating or even an eating disorder. In either case, these people's lives might have been manageable to begin with, and after introducing the addictive behaviors, their lives become unmanageable. It doesn't take long for addictive patterns to develop and for those people to become obsessive about their new lifestyles and new behaviors.

For example, people who have recently lost weight may receive multiple compliments and positive feedback from the people in their lives. For some, this can play into the addictive mindset and fuel the fire for them to continue their weight loss after reaching a healthy, appropriate goal weight—even at the risk of becoming underweight and developing an eating disorder. Once the innocent goal to eat healthy or diet to lose a little weight becomes an obsession, the chance for it to progress into something unhealthy and destructive is possible. Recent statistics on dieting show that 35 percent of normal dieters progress to pathological dieting. Of those, 20–25 percent progress to partial or full-syndrome eating disorders. In an effort to maintain a healthy state—both mentally and physically—the phrase "all things in moderation" definitely applies when considering diet and exercise.

On the other hand, many people turn to addictive behaviors as a way to cope with a life that already feels out of control. There are many underlying issues that can contribute to why someone might turn to substances, pornography, gambling, overeating, or another type of eating disorder. These addictive behaviors can serve as an escape from reality and create a world that seems more carefree, mindless, void of stress, and, ironically, manageable. Typically, people who cope with the stresses of life through addiction or eating disorders are choosing to escape reality, numb out their emotions, and avoid unpleasant and uncomfortable feelings.

Contributing factors that might leave people feeling like they need an escape could include a recent divorce, a death of a loved one, losing a job, not getting into a desired school, past trauma such as abuse or rape, abandonment issues, rejection, or even bullying. This list could go on and on and even include successes in life and happy events that are too overwhelming for people to adjust to.

We all handle stressors in life differently, so it's hard to determine if one life event will have a bigger impact than another. This isn't to say that anyone who experiences an upsetting life event, trauma, or otherwise overwhelming incident will undoubtedly turn to an addiction. It depends on the person, his or her life circumstance, and how he or she understands the way to process and cope with his or her emotions and the world around him or her. Underlying genetics, environmental factors, sociocultural influences, and the ability to learn coping skills can all play a part in how someone responds to less than ideal situations in life.

EMOTIONS

Crying is how your body speaks when your mouth can't explain the pain you feel.

—Unknown

So how do we learn how to process and cope with the world around us? This education begins at a very early age. We watch and learn from those we are closest to and mirror the behaviors we see in others, including how the people around us handle their emotions. Time and time again, I have listened to women with eating disorders describe the home environments they grew up in. Many of them will comment about how they weren't allowed to show emotion or talk about their true feelings in their families. They were brought up to believe that there was something wrong with feeling their emotions and that it was even worse to actually express them.

As a result, the women suppressed and covered up their emotions. In some of their families, emotions and conversations were kept on a very superficial level. These women were taught that they were supposed to be tough and not let people see them sad or crying. And it would be a cold day in hell if they ever saw their parents cry . . . especially their fathers. They've shared that they grew up watching their parents mask emotions and learned from their example.

In many of their families, the women were expected to put on a happy face, smile, and show the world that life was "perfect." They learned to feel bad, shameful, and embarrassed for experiencing natural and normal human emotions. This home environment certainly doesn't apply to every single person with an eating disorder; however, this description of home life and upbringing is common enough to render significance.

Yet, emotions are necessary in understanding and experiencing opposites, something that is of value to everyone regardless of views of religion or spirituality. For example, if we don't learn the difference between hot and cold, there is a good chance that we will get burned at some point in life. This certainly applies to emotions as well. We cannot know happiness without having felt sadness. Life is full of joy and happiness, but we all know sadness, sorrow, and pain. These "unpleasant" emotions are natural and important parts of our life experience.

Many of the greatest life lessons are learned when we experience and truly work through some of the emotions that are perceived to be negative and unacceptable. If you are taught in your childhood and adolescence to ignore, hide, suppress, and devalue those unpleasant emotions, what does that teach you to do later in life when you genuinely feel sad, scared, upset, or disappointed?

People who have been discouraged from expressing their true feelings or who have never learned by example how to handle their emotions in a healthy way can find the ups and downs in life to be very uncomfortable, confusing, and scary. For many people, their only escape is to cover up the sadness, hurt, or disappointment with some form of destructive behavior. Addiction can become the coping skill they learn to use as a way to numb the unwanted and "unacceptable" feelings.

For example, turning to eating disorder behaviors helps people numb out and shut down emotions such as hurt, disappointment, shame, guilt, neglect, loneliness, and fear, just to name a few. For them, engaging in binging, purging, restricting, overexercising, or some other obsessive behavior regarding weight or body image acts as a distraction. Their compulsive behaviors drown out the realities of their emotions and provide a way for them to get by. When the emotions become too much to handle, some people may turn to cutting on their skin as a way to visualize the overwhelming pain and sadness they are feeling inside.

Sadly, these negative behaviors are effective, which is why people continue to go back to the same destructive and unhealthy cycle time after time. At their very core, people understand that what they are doing doesn't make sense. They understand that their behaviors aren't the norm for society and that, to a certain extent, they are out of control; however, that doesn't negate the reality that the addictive behaviors temporarily work. The behaviors serve a purpose and help people to feel better in the moment.

One way to think of eating disorders is to compare them to people in unhealthy relationships. Think for a minute about the people you have known in your life. It's quite possible that you have known people or currently know people who are in unhealthy relationships. Maybe these people are with a partner who belittles them, makes them feel inferior, or who abuses them in some way mentally, emotionally, or physically. Their significant other might even take advantage of them, causing their self-esteem to break down little by little.

No matter how many incidents occur or how sad they feel time after time, they continue to return to the relationship. They are unable to even explain why; they just know that the relationship feels comfortable and safe in a strange way. For those of us on the outside looking in, it might seem crazy that they would keep going back. But for the person on the inside, it might be all he or she knows. For him or her, the thought of leaving and venturing out into the unknown, into new relationships, is terrifying.

Like these relationships, eating disorders are negative, destructive, abusive, and controlling. Yet, at the same time, they offer comfort, relief, and support in a way that nothing and no one else can. People involved in a relationship with Ed may continue to feel degraded, ashamed, and guilty each time they engage in the relationship. But at the same time, they may be too scared, confused, and alone to make a break and try to get away.

In essence, the relationship between people and eating disorders is a bittersweet love. A relationship they hate to love on so many levels because of the negative consequences. Yet they love to hold onto it in order to feel some sense of control and identity in their life. The relationship they begin to hold onto is the illness.

The nature of the illness results in a disconnectedness from meaningful relationships. They connect on a much deeper level with the illness and think they are their compulsive behaviors—it's where they can go in order to disconnect from everything else. Any attempts to let go of this harmful relationship potentially opens the floodgates for all of the emotions and realities of life they are trying so hard to avoid—emotions they have learned so well to suppress in order to function from day to day; however, they may be falling apart on the inside, and would hate for people to notice that they are falling apart on the outside.

It is helpful for parents, guardians, teachers, and other role models to teach children and show them by example that it is okay for them to experience various emotions. Life comes with ups and downs. Not everything is going to go our way or be perfect 100 percent of the time. And that is okay! To put on a façade that people, families, and relationships are always content, happy, and healthy only hurts those involved in the long run. This can encourage people to live in a false reality and deny their genuine thoughts, feelings, and emotions. There is an anonymous quote that states, "If we are in complete control of our family, then somewhere along the way we have gone terribly wrong."

It's difficult to be genuine and real about our lives and the ups and downs that come along with it if we are constantly worried about what people on the outside are thinking. Time and again, people are afraid to show real emotion and to be genuine because they think others will dislike them. In reality, the opposite is often true. Most people appreciate genuineness from others and connect with people on a deeper level when they are willing to be sincere and real about who they are: the good, the bad, and the ugly.

Oftentimes parents will engage with their children during happy and playful times and then try to shield them from seeing them when they are upset. It makes sense on some level to want to protect children from seeing parents in a moment that many would consider to be weak; however, in reality, are parents protecting their children if all they learn from their parents' example is to let others see them only when they are happy? Indirectly, parents may be teaching their children that being sad and crying are unacceptable and that emotions can only be talked about and vocalized if those emotions are positive, lighthearted, and joyful.

It's important to teach children that it is okay to feel happy in life as well as sad. It is okay to laugh when something is funny and to cry when something is hurting. Children and adolescents need to learn and understand that there are certain things in life within their control and certain things that are out of their control. For example, we can control the way we choose to react to people and situations. We can control the way we treat others; however, we can't control the choices in life that other people make or the reaction other people may have in situations and conversations.

Many people with eating disorders try to control this. They have a desire and tendency to avoid conflict and make an effort to please everyone. Their strong desire to be liked and accepted by others leads them to neglecting their own needs and making sure that everyone around them is taken care of first. There is nothing wrong with wanting to be accepted or wanting people to like you, but when your efforts come at the expense of your own well-being, it can create many problems. Over time, taking care of others and continually putting the needs of others first breaks us down until we have nothing left to give.

In no way am I suggesting that we carry about day to day wearing all of our sorrows on our sleeve and having pity parties; however, I would urge you to be genuine and real with those close to you, especially children and adolescents. During these young years they are learning how to express themselves and how to get their needs met in healthy ways. Teach them that it is okay to feel and express emotions, both happy and sad. Show them that you also experience real emotion day to day. Don't be afraid to be honest and open in your communication with them.

In turn, you will teach them that it is okay for them to experience ups and downs, joy and sorrow, happiness and sadness. They will learn to express their emotions in healthy and appropriate ways instead of feeling guilty and not knowing where to turn. It is in not knowing where to turn for support, love, and validation that people may find themselves entrapped in the cycle of addiction.

BODY IMAGE

You are imperfect permanently and inevitably flawed. And you are beautiful.

—Amy Bloom

Our emotions play a significant role in our day-to-day actions and behaviors. The way we think and feel about ourselves—including our bodies—is evident in our daily interactions with the world around us. The mind is a powerful tool. We come to believe the repetitive images and thoughts which enter our minds at a rapid pace each day. If those images and thoughts are such that they cause us to feel negatively about the way we look, it can greatly impact the choices we make. For some people, this negative mindset develops into very unhealthy views about body image and can dramatically increase the likelihood of an eating disorder developing.

Body image is defined as the mental picture we have of our own body and includes the emotional experiences we have about our bodies. How many times have you gotten ready for the day, put on an outfit, looked in the mirror, and then changed your outfit, again and again and again? People in the eating disorder world would refer to this as having a "bad body image day." This is when no matter what you do or what clothes you put on, you just don't feel great about your body, and it doesn't seem to look or feel good in anything. For people who struggle with an eating disorder and, consequently, negative body image, this happens more often than not.

Think back for a minute to your childhood. Imagine that you are at the local carnival, and you enter the fun house with your friends. You walk inside and all of a sudden your face, body, and figure are transformed into silly shapes and sizes. The image in the mirror looks nothing like your real self. You may describe the images you see in the fun house as distorted, stretched, squished, plump, and disproportioned in so many ways. This experience definitely presents unrealistic views of your body. You continue to walk through the fun house, laughing and making jokes about yourself and your friends because you look so silly in the mirrors. You're able to laugh about it because you know as soon as you step out of the fun house your real image will appear and everything will be back to normal.

Now, consider for a moment getting ready for the day and stepping in front of a mirror before heading out of your house. What if, in that moment, the image you saw was similar to something you might see in a fun house mirror? I'd be willing to bet that you wouldn't think it was funny and you wouldn't laugh and make jokes about yourself. You'd likely have a difficult time walking out the door and presenting yourself to the world. You might feel ashamed and disappointed to the point of wanting to crawl back in bed and pull the covers over your head.

For people who struggle with eating disorders, that point of view is called *body dysmorphic disorder*. Body dysmorphic disorder can accompany their illness as a condition in which their perceived image of self is different from reality. They truly believe that the image in the mirror is ugly, fat, disproportioned, disgusting, and unworthy of being loved. In their mind, the image of themselves is large, flabby, and fat. Sadly, this is what they see and this is what they believe to be reality.

This distorted view of self and negative body image can lead to many obsessive behaviors. People engage in these behaviors to affirm what they believe to be true. People with eating disorders are constantly thinking about how their bodies look to themselves and to others. They may wrap their hands and fingers around parts of their bodies as a way to measure size and compare their bodies from day to day. They might "body check" the size of their wrists, legs, upper arms, waist, and other parts of their bodies. They may even use their fingers to pinch the extra skin on their waist, legs, or arms. They may engage in these obsessive behaviors from time to time or excessively when experiencing a "bad body image day."

So why this unhealthy obsession with our bodies, and why is it so prevalent in our society? If you consider the world we live in, it's not surprising that so many people struggle with body image. We are constantly bombarded with airbrushed, unrealistic images of what we are supposed to look like. We pay attention to media, celebrities, and fashion icons. Not only do we pay attention, but we have a tendency to buy into the ideals and images they are selling. We are inundated with messages—both directly and indirectly—about ideal size, shape, clothing, exercise, food, and sexuality.

All of these generate emotions for us and contribute to how we perceive our own bodies. It doesn't seem to matter that the very images we are comparing ourselves to have undergone thousands of dollars' worth of airbrushing. Although the images are impossibly perfect, we still use them as the standard for comparison. We voluntarily beat ourselves up because we can't achieve the impossible or measure up to the unrealistic, beauty-driven society in which we live.

Not only is this frustrating, but it is also very sad and disappointing that so many women base their self-worth on how they compare and measure up to the images they see in media and the number they see on the scale. Whether it's on television, in movies, on the computer, on a billboard, or on the cover of a fashion magazine at the grocery store, the images scream out that women are imperfect and not good enough. A recent study showed that the more time girls spent on Facebook, the more they suffered conditions of bulimia, anorexia, physical dissatisfaction, negative physical self-image, negative approaches to eating, and more of an urge to be on a weight-loss diet.

Another way technology affects young girls is through media images. It is estimated that young girls are exposed to between four and six hundred media images per day. Considering this reality adds another dynamic to the reasons why young girls and women struggle so much with body image. It contributes to why women rarely feel they are good enough. If men are seeing the same images and buying into the same impossible reality of what women are supposed to look like, it adds fuel to an already out-of-control fire. Little by little, beliefs and ideas that men have of what women should look like become skewed and unrealistic. Consequently, this contributes to the great misunderstanding behind the ideals shaping our views of body image today.

The comments and messages women hear—both directly and indirectly—about female bodies are powerful beyond measure, especially the comments made by fathers, brothers, and significant others. I would suggest that those who fall into the mentioned demographics do the women in their lives a favor and *stop* commenting on the appearances of the people, especially women, you see on television, in movies, or even in real life.

Instead of acknowledging and commenting that a woman is fat, thin, pretty, or ugly, talk about how women are smart, talented, funny, caring, and successful. Foster the characteristics and attributes that will make women feel strong and secure about who they are and how they are perceived. Encourage them to become something unique rather than becoming like something or someone else.

IDENTITY

You don't have a soul. You are a soul. You have a body.

—C. S. Lewis

It's fair to say that the inability to regulate and process emotions as well as the way people might perceive their bodies both play significant roles in the development of eating disorders and become a consequence of them. The messages we see and hear on a daily basis become engrained in our minds. Whether positive or negative, we begin to believe repetitive messages. They influence our thoughts and have a direct impact on our behaviors. Addictions, including eating disorders, are obsessive and all consuming. For people struggling and fighting the battle day in and day out, this way of living becomes their identity. It provides comfort, a way for them to cope with or avoid the things in life they would rather not deal with emotionally, mentally, and physically.

You'll hear people who have little understanding about eating disorders say, "Well, why don't they just eat?" The magic question "Why?" is asked over and over by those on the outside looking in. It's difficult, it's deeper, and it's complicated on so many levels that most people can't just stop on their own. As crazy as it may seem, the eating disorder becomes what they identify with the most. It consumes their lives to the extent that they honestly don't know or understand who they would be without it.

They have suppressed feelings, emotions, personality, and character to the point of nonexistence. They may have let go of their passions and fully embraced the disorder. People who may have identified in the past with being mothers, daughters, friends, dancers, pianists, writers, or artists have a clouded vision of where that person now exists. Oftentimes, they learn to identify with the eating disorder in a more intimate way than they do with being a person.

Ask people who are trapped in the cycle of addiction to describe who they are as a person and they will likely be at a loss for words. They truly have lost sight of their individual worth, their unique talents, and the beautiful characteristics that make them who they are. They experience themselves as being empty and hollow. They must learn how to cope in healthy ways with the ups and downs of life, allowing the opportunity to discover who they are and embrace the person who was lost along the way.

REFERENCES

"Eating Disorder Statistics & Research." Eating Disorder Hope. Accessed September 16, 2013. http://www.eatingdisorderhope.com/information/statistics-studies#Dieting-Statistics-and-Prevalence.

Hawkins, Nicole. "Battling Our Bodies: Understanding and Overcoming Negative Body Images." Center for Change, Inc. Accessed September 11, 2013. https://www.centerforchange.com/content/battling-our-bodies-understanding-and-overcoming-negative-body-images.

University of Haifa. "Facebook Users More Prone to Developing Eating Disorders, Study Finds." Science Daily. Accessed September 16, 2013. http://www.sciencedaily.com/releases/2011/02/110207091754.htm?utm_source=feedburner&utm_medium=feed&utm_campaign=Feed%3A+sciencedaily%2Fhealth_medicine%2Feating_disorders+(ScienceDaily%3A+Health+%26+Medicine+News+--+Eating+Disorders).

CHAPTER NINE

a new way of coping

Do one thing every day that scares you.

—Eleanor Roosevelt

It has been my observation that people struggling with eating disorders have a difficult time being real and genuine in expressing their feelings. Instead, they suppress their emotions and stuff their feelings to the point of causing emotional, physical, and mental stress. They turn to their compulsive behaviors as a way to release or numb their emotions as well as to escape reality. Engaging in these behaviors might not help them feel good, but this way of coping with life feels better than experiencing emotions that are too difficult to face.

People who have become entrenched in these behaviors adopt them as a way of life and live them in a rigid fashion each day. They have a hard time imagining their lives without them even though they may truly have a need and desire to give up the behaviors. The fear of the unknown holds a lot of people back from seeking help and recovering from their eating disorder. Only one in ten people with eating disorders receives treatment. Eighty percent of the girls or women who have accessed care for their eating disorders do not get the intensity of treatment they need to stay in recovery—they are often sent home weeks earlier than the recommended stay. This statistic is unsettling because the healing process takes time. Unfortunately, many of those who do seek treatment are unable to benefit from long-term care.

HEALING THROUGH TREATMENTS

There are many treatment options for women seeking to recover from the illness. The most effective and long-lasting treatment for an eating disorder is some form of psychotherapy or psychological counseling, coupled with careful attention to medical and nutritional needs. Because eating disorders affect the whole person, it's important for treatment to encompass emotional, mental, spiritual, physical, and social needs. Those in treatment have a long road ahead of them. Unlearning negative behaviors and learning how to cope in positive and healthy ways takes much time.

If you have ever been in the position to completely alter the way you do something in your life, then you might have a very small idea of what it might be like for someone considering treatment. Think of something in your life that helps you alleviate stress or find comfort. Examples could be walking, journaling, baking, playing with pets, or being in nature. Whatever the outlet is for you, consider for a moment being told that you no longer have access to that activity and that you need to replace it with something new. Or, to take it even further, imagine that the most important and comforting relationship in your life is at risk of being taken away.

In general, people don't like change and might even be fearful of it. We tend to like things that are comfortable and familiar. For those struggling with an eating disorder, the illness is what feels comfortable and familiar in their life. The eating disorder has become the most important and comforting relationship for them. Seeking treatment, being open to the idea of recovery, and making changes in the way they cope is terrifying for people engrained in the eating disorder mentality. In reality, they are embarking on a journey where all of their comforts will be taken away and replaced with ways of coping that initially feel foreign, scary, and uncomfortable.

A significant part of the healing process is figuring out what those with the eating disorders enjoy doing and what makes them feel happy. My observation has been that it is necessary to discover healthy coping skills they can turn to when life feels overwhelming instead of turning to eating disorder behaviors. So many people lose sight of their true passions while struggling with addiction that they don't even remember what it is they enjoy. A treatment approach that includes exploring a variety of leisure and recreational options can be extremely beneficial for those learning how to cope in positive ways. It's important for them to learn that there are things in life which will bring enjoyment, pleasure, and comfort without being destructive and avoidant.

Along with rediscovering passions, it can be helpful for people to really look at the reasons why they enjoy doing a particular activity. In general, when people are asked about ways in which they choose to cope with stress, it's not uncommon for them to rattle off a list of sports or other forms of exercise; however, when working with people who have an eating disorder, it's essential to recognize that their reason for exercising or playing sports may stem from unhealthy motives. This can be a tricky part of recovery for many people to face and truly be honest about.

I've known many women who, throughout the course of treatment, have discovered that their reasons for exercising—especially running— are driven by their eating disorder. They obsess about the activity and how many calories it can burn instead of enjoying the movement or the environment in which they run. For them, that exercise serves one purpose and one purpose only: to aid the eating disorder and obsessive thoughts about losing weight.

This realization is a red flag for them in the way they will need to approach running in recovery. Oftentimes, when serious about their recovery, they opt out of running all together. They come to recognize that it's not something they can have a healthy relationship with because the risk is too great. Keep in mind that the example about running is just that—an example. Running could be replaced with anything that is taken to the extreme and used as an accomplice to the eating disorder. For some people it may be running, while for others it may be swimming, dancing, playing soccer, biking, or doing other activities.

While people are in treatment, the focus needs to be on discovering what feels good and healthy for their bodies. For those who have spent so much time and effort hating their bodies and abusing them on many levels, it can be difficult for them to learn how to love their bodies and appreciate the amazing things their bodies can do. Focusing on exercise because it is enjoyable, because it helps to relieve stress or anxiety, or because it makes the body feel good can be beneficial ways to approach physical activities while in recovery. Moderation of exercise is essential to avoid triggers and to battle the eating disorder mindset.

One suggestion for people who have the desire to heal is to generate an ongoing list of positive coping skills. It's important that the list is realistic and includes things that they will actually utilize when needed as well as activities that can help distract from the eating disorder thoughts and urges. These should be enjoyable activities that help foster the recovery mindset as opposed to keeping someone stuck in the eating disorder mentality. Some suggestions of enjoyable activities follow (you may want to try adding a few ideas of your own to this list).

- Take a leisurely walk
- Call or visit a friend
- Volunteer or participate in service activities
- Listen to music
- Read a book
- Color, draw, paint, or do other expressive art activities
- Meditate or practice yoga
- Try deep breathing
- Write in a journal
- Play a game
- Play with a pet
- Take a bubble bath
- Watch a movie
- Paint your fingernails
- Sit or lay outside
- Write a positive letter to yourself or someone significant in your life
- Read or write positive affirmations (tape them up around your house and in your car)
- Go for a drive
- Knit, sew, or crochet

- Go window shopping
- Take a bike ride
- Work in the yard or mow the lawn
- Do a crossword or jigsaw puzzle
- Laugh . . . or cry
- Play with a child
- Focus on spirituality through reading, writing, prayer, yoga, or meditation

Keep in mind that we all react to stress differently. Just because a particular coping skill works for one person doesn't mean that it will work for everyone. This is true of people in recovery as well. That's why it is so important throughout the process of healing to be exposed to a wide variety of positive ways of coping. The more options there are, the easier it will be for people to discover what works best for them.

I would challenge anyone reading this to create your own personal list of positive coping skills. Make an effort and take the time to use them in your life. We all deserve to engage in activities that are enjoyable and fulfilling, especially on days when things seem a little too difficult, busy, or challenging to bear.

BREAKING THE CYCLE OF EATING DISORDERS

Think of a time in your life when you've had a bad day. Chances are that you chalked it up to a bad day and moved on. For many people, simply having a bad day is just that—a bad day. You may choose to make the day a little better by doing something fun or taking a break. The day comes and goes and there is hope for having a better day tomorrow. People who can regulate their emotions and see past the immediate circumstance might go for a walk, read a book, or engage in a favorite hobby, all with the hope of turning the bad day around or making it a little bit better.

A bad day isn't so easily turned around for people who are accustomed to utilizing destructive behaviors as a way to cope. In their minds, when they experience an upset or disappointment, it can be too overwhelming for them to deal with it. They may have no idea how to handle the dissatisfaction of something not going their way or not going as planned. As we learned earlier, eating disorders can become, over time, a way to gain some sense of control. If people find life circumstances to be unpleasant and out of their control, they know they can turn to eating disorder behaviors as a way to feel in control again. Life can be crazy, but they know in the comfort of their eating disorder world that they can escape the noise and focus only on their behaviors.

When people are in the middle of their eating disorder, they turn to destructive behaviors to cope with difficulties in life. As a result, their engagement in these behaviors leaves them feeling low and unhappy and disappointed in themselves. In order to deal with feeling low and unhappy, they once again turn to their negative ways of coping to feel a temporary high and release of emotion. And so the addictive cycle goes, round and round and round.

In order to break this cycle, they must learn new ways of dealing with the vast emotions and circumstances experienced in life. Their brains have been wired to immediately turn to their negative ways of coping, so it happens naturally; they don't have to think too much about it. It's like when you experience an itch on your skin; you immediately reach to scratch it in order to make the irritating feeling go away. Emotions for people struggling with an eating disorder can be thought of like an itch. Their immediate reaction is to get rid of the feeling by using the behaviors that have proven to work for them time and time again. Just as drug addicts have urges to use drugs, those with eating disorders have urges to engage in their compulsive behaviors, such as binging, purging, restricting, cutting, overexercising, and obsessing about body image. When the urges come, they can be all-consuming, and it can be very difficult for those engaging in the behaviors to focus on anything else.

I have witnessed many women in the process of recovering from an eating disorder try to be patient with urges and address them in healthy ways, using positive coping skills, instead of automatically resorting to negative behaviors. This new way of reacting to urges is a lot easier said than done. Next time you have an itch on your skin, resist the urge to scratch it. Likely, this will drive you crazy and you will be unable to think about anything else.

The good news is that urges—like itches—do pass. Many people who are trying to overcome addictions are encouraged to sit with it—sit with their emotions, sit with the urges to act on triggers and allow them the time to pass. Sit with the urges for fifteen minutes. If they are still there after that amount of time, sit with them for another fifteen minutes. This takes great patience, willpower, and the ability to focus on the genuine desired outcomes pertaining to recovery.

CHANGING THE RELATIONSHIP WITH FOOD

One area in which those struggling with eating disorders have to learn new skills and ways of coping has to do specifically with their relationship with food. Obviously, this illness involves unhealthy thoughts, beliefs, and behaviors about food. The disadvantage for people with eating disorders is that food is a part of everyday life. We need food to survive and function properly. Our bodies need to be nourished and fed sufficiently. People who struggle with a drug addiction can avoid their substances and still survive. People with eating disorders don't have that option.

It doesn't help that food is everywhere. It is at the center of most social gatherings and pretty difficult to escape altogether. How often do you hear people say, "We should meet for lunch and catch up"? That's likely the last thing people with an eating disorder want to hear. When it comes to gatherings of family and friends, birthdays, holidays, or simple day-to-day socializing, food plays a significant role. Just think of how stressful this might be for people with unhealthy ways of interacting with and being around food.

Food is an inevitable, essential part of life. This makes it very difficult when beginning the journey of recovery. There has to be a focus on making peace with food. Whether the people are engaged in the binge or purge cycle or have a tendency to restrict calories, their relationship with food is an unhealthy one.

As a society, we put moral values on food. Cookies are "bad" and veggies are "good." The key to abolishing the pattern of restraint and subsequent overeating is to give yourself unconditional permission to eat. This means throwing out the preconceived notion that certain foods are good and others are bad. No one food has the power to make you fat or help you become slim.

The reality is that food isn't good or bad; food is food. It's meant to be enjoyable and to provide nourishment. There is nothing wrong with people finding pleasure in eating a piece of cake or having a pasta dinner. Yet, as a society, we make guilt-producing statements about our choices in food almost daily. We put moral values on the food we eat, which in turn impacts the way we perceive ourselves as humans based on what we eat: either good or bad. When you think about it, this is quite silly—to let eating pieces of cake determine if we are a good or bad person. How about allowing ourselves to be a great person who simply enjoys cake!

People in recovery will definitely need support from those around them to help them have a more positive relationship with food. If the people in their lives are obsessed with the idea of good and bad foods and eating low-fat, fat-free, or carbohydrate-free food, it will be difficult for them to avoid having eating disorder thoughts. Being surrounded by people who entertain unhealthy ways of viewing food or exercise can be a strong trigger for people in recovery. It's a slippery slope; little by little the attitudes and behaviors of loved ones can spark the negative thoughts that contribute to the eating disorder.

There are many things that family and friends can do to help their loved ones have success in recovery. These things will allow them to use their positive coping skills as opposed to feeling triggered in their home environments. Here are some suggestions:

- Avoid dieting—it is inevitable that when people diet they obsess about and talk about food (and whether it's good or bad) constantly.
- Avoid having "diet" food in the house. Enjoy a variety of foods when you are hungry and stop eating when you are full.
- Eat meals and snacks with your loved ones, and eat the same thing they are eating.
- Get rid of the scale! The number on the scale doesn't define who you are as a person.
- Don't subscribe to or buy fashion magazines. Viewing this type of media and comparing ourselves to airbrushed images leads to negative thoughts and feelings about our bodies.

- Avoid talking about food as either good or bad. Food doesn't have a moral value.
- Don't save "skinny" clothes. If you do, you inadvertently send the message that you are unhappy with yourself and need to lose weight. Instead, embrace who you are.
- Participate in physical activities and exercise for the sake of being healthy, enjoying movement, and having fun; try to avoid exercising specifically to burn calories.

Subscribing to the diet mentality is powerful and can lead to many negative consequences. Obviously, parents aren't perfect, and it is common for them to struggle with their own issues surrounding food and body image. In fact, being a parent is arguably one of the most difficult roles we can take on. There is a great sense of responsibility to be positive examples for our children, since children have a tendency to model the behaviors they see in their parents. It's wonderful to know that awareness and education can change the way we speak with our children and behave around them. Parents can learn how to positively influence their children's perceptions of food and body image related issues, therefore contributing to the development of positive self-esteem and body image throughout their lives.

LEARNING HOW TO ASK FOR HELP

By nature, many people with eating disorders tend to be people pleasers. They are concerned with the well-being of others and want to make sure that those around them are happy and taken care of. While this sounds admirable, it can actually become quite destructive and unhealthy when they no longer put their needs above anyone else.

Do you remember reading about Kristin's need to be accepted? She wanted so much to be liked and loved by those around her that she put her needs and emotions aside in favor of making others happy. She wrote, "I feel like I have to act like I 'used to be.' Some people don't like me because they say I am no fun anymore . . . I don't really know who I am."

In this effort to please everyone around them, people with eating disorders continuously avoid their own needs emotionally, physically, and mentally. They would never want to put someone else out or be a burden.

Because of this, people who struggle with eating disorders may have a very difficult time asking for help. For many, learning how to ask for help is probably the most difficult coping skill they have to embrace in recovery. They are so used to being alone in their illness that it might feel very uncomfortable and awkward to speak up and express a need for help.

The truth of the matter is that recovery requires help, love, and support from close family and friends. It's important for those leaving the eating disorder world and embarking on the road to recovery to identify someone they feel they can approach when they need support. Even if it's just to say, "Hey, I'm having a hard time and struggling right now with eating disorder thoughts." Sometimes just being able to vocalize a need for extra support is enough to help lift the burden the eating disorder thoughts put on them. Being able to ask for help in recovery also holds that someone accountable and prevents the topic from being taboo.

Honest communication is a vital part of recovery. Those in recovery need to be held accountable and those helping their loved ones in recovery need to be able to hold them accountable. It's OK to ask questions and open the door for honest communication to take place about how they are thinking, feeling, and acting. This doesn't mean you bombard them with twenty questions each day and hover over their every move, but it is important for them to know that they have a safe place where they can express their needs, cope in positive ways, and ask for help.

GETTING THROUGH RELAPSES

Learning how to cope with eating disorders in healthy ways and making an effort to avoid destructive behaviors is difficult and takes practice. Nobody is going to cope with life perfectly 100 percent of the time. Throughout the recovery process there can be a lot of ups and downs that may include setbacks, most commonly referred to as relapses. Relapses are a normal part of the process and do not equate to failure. Nobody is perfect in this life and certainly nobody is perfect in recovery. However, over time and with a lot of practice, people can become better and better in recovery.

The idea that relapse is part of recovery can be a difficult concept for those close to the people suffering. Although relapse can be discouraging, this kind of setback is certainly *not* a sign of failure. As mentioned, recovery is a process. Relapse, as well as how people recover from relapse, is part of the learning that takes place along the way. It's important for family and friends to focus less on the actual relapse and more on what their loved one does to get back on track following the relapse.

This isn't to say that a relapse shouldn't be addressed; a relapse can be a valuable learning tool and a red flag that some adjustments in recovery need to be made. Something to focus on could be how quickly they are willing to be honest about the relapse, when in the past they would have tried so hard to hide their behaviors. Focus on their willingness to let people in and ask for help. Focus on the things they are doing well and then make an effort to move forward and be supportive.

COPING IN HEALTHY WAYS

So how does the process of learning how to cope in healthy ways begin? The answer is slowly. Recovery doesn't happen overnight. It can take six months, one year, or many years. Recovery is a lifelong process that begins with a single decision to seek help. This decision is then followed by the daily decision to keep fighting, make different choices, and move forward in recovery. One of the simplest ways I've heard women in recovery describe their new way of coping is, "When the eating disorder is telling me to do something, I do the exact opposite!"

In no way am I implying that this is simple to do. Recovery takes an enormous amount of strength and hope for a better future—a future freed from the eating disorder. In recovery it is important to continue the fight against eating disorders. The eating disorders trigger thoughts, feelings, emotions, and urges, and these triggers can still be strong even after abstaining from the behaviors for an extended period of time. Some valuable recovery tools that come with time are being mindful of the negative thoughts and having the ability to distinguish the eating disorder mindset from the rational, healthy mindset. A few examples of doing the opposite of what Ed (a personification of eating disorders) is telling you to do are follow:

- If Ed tells you to skip a meal or snack—*eat it anyway.*
- If Ed tells you that an outfit makes you look fat—*wear it anyway.*

- If Ed tells you to run an extra mile because it will burn more calories— *stop running.*
- If Ed tells you that you are too ugly to be seen in public—*go out anyway.*
- If Ed tells you that you aren't smart enough to apply for college or a job—*apply anyway.*
- If Ed tells you that nobody cares about you or loves you enough to help—*ask for help.*
- If Ed tells you to keep a secret—*be honest and open in your communication.*
- If Ed tells you that you can't wear a swimsuit—*put it on and go swimming.*
- If Ed tells you that you don't deserve to eat dessert— *eat and enjoy dessert.*
- If Ed tells you to run off the dessert you just ate—*don't run.*
- If Ed tells you that you simply aren't good enough to do something—*do it anyway.*
- If Ed tells you that you can't go out to dinner with a friend—*go out to dinner.*
- If Ed tells you you're fat and worthless—*pray to know your worth.*
- If Ed tells you that you are not beautiful, you may just need to laugh at Ed and tell him that you know you're awesome and that you're working on believing that *you are beautiful.*

REFERENCES

National Eating Disorders Association (NEDA). Accessed May 30, 2014. www.nationaleatingdisorders.org.

South Carolina Department of Mental Health. "Eating Disorder Statistics." Accessed September 16, 2013. hypp://www.state.sc.us/dmh/anorexia/statistics.htm.

Tribole, Evelyn, and Elyse Resch. Intuitive Eating: A Revolutionary Program that Works (ital). New York: St. Martin's Griffin, 2003, 84.

CHAPTER TEN

beautiful is . . .

Happy girls are the prettiest.

—Audrey Hepburn

It has been said that beauty is in the eye of the beholder. If this statement is true, then it suggests that everything and everyone in this life is beautiful to someone. This would mean that just because you or I don't find something or someone particularly beautiful doesn't mean that the very same object or person wouldn't be considered beautiful in someone else's eyes. What a wonderful and refreshing thought: we are all beautiful to someone!

Take, for example, the birth of a baby. Now, let's be honest—there can be some not-so-cute babies when they are very first born. Nevertheless, if you ask the parents of any newborn, they will tell you over and over and over how beautiful and sweet their new little baby is. Again, beauty is in the eye of the beholder. And thank goodness for that in the case of newborn babies! In that moment at birth, they are unconditionally loved, no matter what color their hair is, the pigment of their skin, or the shape of their head and face. Sadly, the same unconditional love is not granted by peers, society, or sometimes even loved ones as they grow and become integrated into the harsh world in which we live.

At a very early age, children start to recognize the differences they see in people—the way they dress, the color of their hair, the color of their skin, whether or not they have freckles, and whether they are skinny or overweight, just to name a few. The funny thing about children is that they will talk about the things they see about people and point out the things that they have questions about. The comments and questions children start to have about people and their appearances turn into important teaching moments for parents and guardians. These moments are those that, based on the responses of parental figures, will begin to shape the kids' perception of how people should or shouldn't look.

On a daily basis, we are constantly being told what beauty is and what it should look like. I think it's fair to say that by Western culture and media-driven standards, beauty is only skin deep. What you see on the outside defines the person you'll get on the inside. Snap judgments are made all of the time as a result of outward appearances. Despite the saying, "Don't judge a book by its cover," people judge other people by their "cover" every day. What a sad reality that our entire identity can be perceived by another person in a matter of seconds, solely based on how we might look on a particular day without them ever having the opportunity to or taking the time to really get to know us as individuals.

When the world tells us how to define or perceive beauty, it takes away from the idea that beauty truly lies within the eye of the beholder. This outward influence persuades us to conform to another person's or group's or marketer's ideal and definition of beauty. This in turn results in us being less in line with who we really are and what we truly value. We learn to adopt the opinions and views of others instead of believing we are capable of recognizing beauty on our own when we see it.

As a society, we conform to the constricted view of defining beauty by the images we see in entertainment and fashion magazines. In reality, media is selling self-doubt, low self-esteem, and negative body image. Yet we continue to buy and believe their messages regarding beauty time and time again, instead of distinguishing for ourselves what beauty is. Over time and little by little, we are being robbed of our ability to form opinions based on our own thoughts. We become desensitized to the fact that our mind processes and interprets images that have been manipulated to "perfection" and defined by someone else as beautiful.

There are many reasons why we consider things to be beautiful. Maybe a particular person or place makes us feel happy and in our minds that equates to being beautiful. Maybe we have grown so close to other people that we recognize their true beauty as it radiates from the inside to the outside. Maybe some things or people are simply beautiful, but by what standard of measurement is this determined? Is it based on their outward appearance, what kind of clothes they wear, or how they style their hair? Or is it based on how they treat others, or whether or not they are kind, loving, and confident? Stop and think about this for a moment: how do *you* actually define beauty?

A recent study found that only 2 percent of thousands of women from ten countries around the world consider themselves beautiful. This sad and disturbing statistic would suggest that we either live in a world where women are simply not beautiful, or we have a massive and immediate need for a new and more realistic definition of what beauty is. It is time to take a stand and stop equating beauty to the definitions we are shown through media, entertainment, television, magazines, fashion runways, and celebrities.

In a acceptance speech at the Teen Choice Awards, a well-known and very popular actor, Ashton Kutcher, did just this; he took a stand. He went outside of mainstream Hollywood to actually express his own opinions and beliefs about how young people today view important aspects of life, including being beautiful and sexy. This type of gesture is not the norm for actors who are so immersed in the unrealistic vanity of the world. He made one point, specifically, which stands out above all of the rest: "The sexiest thing in the entire world is being really smart."

Notice Ashton Kutcher didn't say that the sexiest thing in the entire world was having the latest fashions to wear, looking like models in fashion magazines, or being like celebrities on the big screen. He didn't mention weighing too much or too little or wearing a certain size. He didn't mention body types: being short or tall, having an athletic build, or having a lean body. He didn't talk about skin, eye, or hair color. He didn't talk about whether or not a woman has curves or fake breasts or wears high heels. He simply stated that being sexy equates to being really smart. What a powerful, meaningful, and relevant statement for people of all ages to hear.

This insight and opinion means even more coming from a very

successful celebrity in Hollywood, an environment which floods us daily with the exact opposite message. What he did, and more importantly what he said, is admirable. Messages just like his that go against the stereotypical views of beauty are needed in order for the perceptions and unrealistic expectations surrounding beauty to change.

Can you imagine if there were more influential people in the world who used their platforms to speak out against the obsession with vanity as we know it today? Can you imagine how much healthier the perceptions of beauty and body image would be if there were more people taking a stand and focusing on the characteristics that make us who we are as individuals?

The world would be a much different place, a place where people—especially women—would be given "permission" to be comfortable in their own skin. They wouldn't have to worry or feel the pressure to compare themselves to every other person they see. Just imagine a world where women as a whole are empowered to feel confident and embrace their true beauty, a beauty all their own that doesn't need to be measured up to celebrities, models, or even the peers they associate with. It would be a beauty all their own—imperfectly perfect.

This ideal world where women of all ages can be truly free from the negative, constant chatter surrounding body image can begin to grow among peers and in families. Parents are encouraged to compliment their daughters on their true beauty—their inner talents and characteristics that define them as a person and not just the image in a mirror. Parents should recognize and speak of their daughters' gifts as people, their ability to be compassionate, their ability to be a leaders, their intelligence, and their ability to be a good, loyal friends. Bequeath confidence to them in areas other than physical appearance.

Remember that our minds are powerful and that we believe the messages we hear over and over again. If your children are hearing more messages about their appearance than any other characteristics or talents they possess, then they will naturally come to believe that appearance is the important thing to focus on. If you are repeatedly bringing up their looks or the appearance of others, then they will learn that their appearance is the one thing that will get most of your desired attention. They will do it even if it means going to extreme measures, like developing an eating disorder. They will do whatever it takes to ensure they focus time and energy on the one thing they've learned to identify with. Help your children form their identities around things that are truly meaningful and important as opposed to vanity and appearances.

In writing this book, I spoke with men, women, and children of all ages about their ideas and definitions of beauty. I found that the responses varied depending on gender and age. It is very telling to see the impact that media and society have on children and teens when it comes to their perceptions of beauty. It might surprise parents to know just how easily influenced their young children are by outside influences. Again, stressing the importance of and addressing the topics of self-esteem, self-worth, body image, and true beauty in the home are important to do, especially when children are young.

It's no wonder that the older and wiser people are, the more realistic and compassionate their definition of beauty becomes. When children are forming their ideas of how people "should" look and what it is about a person that makes them beautiful, they're likely to conform to the narrow views portrayed in media. Their ideas and opinions are simply swayed by the world around them. Imagine if there didn't have to be a waiting period and life experience in order for people to recognize true, genuine beauty. If at an early age children were taught to focus less on vanity and more on what beauty is, they would learn to appreciate and respect others for who they really are on the inside.

The following responses come from personal interviews I conducted. They suggest that definitions of beauty become more meaningful over time and with more life experience:

> *Beautiful is . . . Mommy.*
> —male, age 3

> *The way someone dresses and the way they do their hair.*
> —male, age 8

Beautiful is someone pretty who wears cute clothes and has pretty hair.

—female, age 10

Beautiful means someone who is pretty.

—male, age 11

Beautiful is someone who is pretty, confident, and wears appropriate clothing.

—female, age 12

Beauty is to have compassion in your face.

—male, age 13

Having a good personality makes a person more beautiful.

—female, age 15

Confidence makes a person beautiful.

—female, age 15

A beautiful person possesses the light of Christ and loves everyone. They smile a lot and make others happy.

—female, age 15

A beautiful person has integrity and good personal standards. [He or she doesn't] care what other people think of [him or her].

—female, age 15

Beautiful means to have good looks and personality.

—male, age 16

Confidence and really knowing who [he or she is] as a person makes someone beautiful.

—female, age 28

There is nothing more beautiful than [people] who [are] truly happy. They radiate something that, no matter what shape or size, is the truest form of beauty.

—female, age 29

[People are] beautiful once you get to know and understand who they truly are. The intimacy of completing each other's thoughts is a beautiful thing. All the unspoken nuances and small understandings that two people share together. Everything else is just superficial, and superficial beauty never lasts. It has to go deeper. What makes [people]

beautiful is simply getting to know them as individual[s].
—male, age 30

Being comfortable with who you are and feeling confident is beautiful!
—female, age 35

Beauty is the act of pushing ourselves to become better people. Someone who gives to others but remembers to give to self—that is beautiful!
—female, age 35

Beautiful is someone who is healthy, confident, and comfortable in [his or her] own skin; someone who strives to be kind, loving, and accepting of other people. Beauty cannot be bought at the store—it comes from within.
—female, age 35

Beautiful is genuinely knowing and loving who you are—this exudes confidence.
—female, age 36

Someone who recognizes true beauty in others is in turn beautiful. [His or her] soul is tender, loving, and compassionate. There are no characteristics more beautiful.
—female, age 36

A sense of humor and self-confidence. If people have the ability to make others laugh, it's likely that they're laughing too; that makes [people] beautiful. If [people] have the self-confidence to not care what others think about them regardless of their status in life, career, religious or political views, outward appearance, and so many more of the everyday judgments people tend to pass on others, then that makes [people] beautiful!
—male, age 37

What makes a person beautiful is having self-confidence and self-worth. Being a good person who is not self-absorbed is beautiful. Also, someone who takes pride in [his or her] appearance and is physically fit exudes beauty.
—male, age 37

A strong, smart, confident woman is beautiful.
—male, age 37

Beautiful is someone who is positive, helps others, smiles often, and loves life!

—female, age 38

People are beautiful as a result of who they are in their heart. Beauty is more than what you see on the outside.

—female, age 45

A beautiful person genuinely cares for others and tries to help them when [he or she] can.

—female, age 60

Someone who is beautiful gives of [his or her self] and helps others.

—male, age 62

Beauty is a caring heart and a compassionate, gentle spirit.

—male, age 66

The real beauty of a person is not what we see but what we feel. Mother Teresa would not be considered "beautiful" by the world's standard of beauty; however, her real beauty was on the inside and the person that she was; the selfless way she lived her life made all who knew her or knew of her feel her goodness. That is what makes a person "beautiful."

—female, age 67

If we are striving each day to be kinder to others, then our inner beauty grows and we become beautiful on the outside as well. To be more beautiful on the outside requires us to be beautiful on the inside.

—female, age 88

The statements above make it clear that perception of beauty changes over time. Imagine a young girl, impressed upon by the messages of the media telling her that she must look perfect, wear certain clothes, and have just the right hairstyle. Imagine how fragile she is and how quickly self-esteem and body image can be negatively impacted if she is never told why she is beautiful. I don't mean reasons having to do with her appearance or choice of style when it comes to clothing and hair. A young girl needs to know that she is beautiful from within.

In this book we have heard many of Kristin's family members and friends commenting that they just wish they had been able to communicate to her how beautiful she was, and not because she was thin. They wished that she could have understood that her beauty was in her kindness, her humor, and her deep sense of love. This is the message we hope to communicate with this book.

The truth is that beauty is not only skin deep. It's much deeper than what someone looks like on the surface. True beauty emanates from someone's soul and from touching lives in ways beyond measure. When we are enhancing our inner beauty, our outer beauty is enhanced tenfold. An environment where inner beauty can be enhanced is what young women in the world today need. They hear enough about their outer beauty from all of the worldly influences that scream at them daily.

The home, filled with family and friends, is the perfect place and opportunity for true beauty to flourish. Granted, it's wonderful and helps build self-esteem for teens to hear from their parents and loved ones that they look beautiful. But if this is the only message they are hearing on a regular basis, then the chances of them focusing on much else begins to fade away. Cultivating confidence on many levels is imperative for the healthy development of self-esteem. Likewise, positive self-esteem helps to boost confidence. Young women with healthy self-esteem will be less likely to resort to eating disorder behaviors as a way to cope with life.

REFERENCES

PR Newswire. "Only Two Percent of Women Describe Themselves as Beautiful: New Global Study Uncovers Desire for Broader Definition of Beauty." Accessed September 28, 2013. http://www.prnewswire. com/news-releases/only-two-percent-of-women-describe-them- selves-as-beautiful-73980552.html.

PART 3

Joy of Recovery

CHAPTER ELEVEN

there is hope: life after an eating disorder

The good news is that recovery from an eating disorder is possible. Not everyone's story needs to end as Kristin's did. While it's important to discuss and be aware of the devastating realities of this illness, it is also very important to focus on hope and healing. Many people do and will continue to overcome this illness. The light at the end of the tunnel can be found and it can carry struggling individuals to a place of healing and recovery. This chapter will share a story of courage, hope, healing, and recovery.

The following story describes the experiences of a Becky Berry. Here, she tells her story in an effort to help others who may be struggling with eating disorders. Although the road to recovery can look very different for each individual, the value in sharing Becky's story comes in the overall message that recovery is possible. Becky was a young girl when she began her relationship with Ed but has since become a woman with the desire to help others defeat Ed.

BECKY'S STORY

Can you really recover from an eating disorder? Does the eating disorder always remain a part of you? Is it something you forever have to be careful with and mindful of? What if something traumatic happens in your life and you have no other way of coping? Can you overcome thinking about your body image all of the time? These are questions I used to ask myself often. These questions seemed overwhelming and impossible to really find the answers to.

Fat and ugly were words that plagued my mind for many minutes of every day. Food, weight, self-worth, body image, and negative thoughts were what I thought about 90 percent of the time. It didn't matter whether I was at work, at school, or at home—the thoughts were there. The eating disorder was in the middle of every relationship and it encompassed everything I loved and hated. It was lurking, just waiting to take over.

I felt in control at the beginning; I could turn it on and off. I was often complimented for my strength and self-control. Many people would say, "I wish I had some of your self-control so I could lose *x* amount of pounds." What none of us realized was that the self-control accompanied by self-hate almost destroyed me and took my life.

It began when I was a little girl. I grew up in the Bay Area, living in a wealthy town without much wealth. Innately, I was a very sensitive child. I could feel greater joy, but I could also feel greater hurt and sorrow. What some would've taken with a grain of salt, I took to heart. All of the little remarks said by teachers, friends, and parents struck me to the core and made me strive to be a better person. I wanted to be perfect; however, I had no idea what perfect meant.

I can't remember many moments when I felt good enough, nice enough, or smart enough. I longed to feel loved and to be accepted. I would never say anything that might hurt anyone else's feelings, and I made a conscious effort to be liked by everyone. I was a people pleaser. I didn't want anyone to be hurt or be sad. And if they were hurt or sad I wanted to help them feel better. My saving grace as a child was humor. I learned this at a young age and used it to deal with pain as well as to mask my feelings and emotions.

My eating disorder began at age twelve, when people who were supposed to be building my self-esteem told me that I was too fat, and they were embarrassed to be around me. During this same time, I also had dance teachers and peers telling me that I was too fat. I learned from a very young age, in my mind, that who you are as a person depends on your appearance. I know now how incorrect that mindset is. It took me years to learn the truth.

My parents were going through a divorce at the time, and home was not a pleasant place for me to be. I began coping with my emotions by overeating. I knew that I needed to be healthier, but the more I concentrated on restricting my food intake, the more I wanted to eat. I remember being told not to eat certain foods because they would make me fat, and fat was not acceptable in my paradigm. A couple of years passed, and I had gained several pounds. I hated my body, I hated myself, and I hated my life.

My dance teacher threatened that if I didn't lose a significant amount of weight, I would not be in the elite dance group the following season. Again, it was reinforced that who I was as a person depended on my appearance and the number on the scale. I remember the day she told me this very clearly. I was at her house with a bunch of my dance friends. With no discreteness whatsoever, she told me that I was too fat and I needed to lose weight to be in the elite dance group next year. I was so humiliated, so embarrassed, and I felt totally worthless.

I decided to take all of these comments to heart and began watching what I ate. I wanted so badly to be included as part of the elite dance group. I made an effort to eat more balanced and became more active. As I began to exercise moderately and decrease my emotional eating, I began to naturally become closer to my set point. A set point is where your body naturally wants to be when you are listening to what you are truly hungry for and balancing moderate exercise. It was working! I was being accepted and began to recognize that people noticed me. I received a lot of encouragement to continue trying to be healthy.

Soon after the initial weight loss, my body hit a plateau—my set point. It was then that I began to exhibit unhealthy behaviors. I wasn't giving my body the nutrition that it needed. I didn't realize that I had begun an addiction that was going to be very difficult to stop. Thinking about food and my body consumed me. Quickly, these thoughts began to creep into my every action. I was rapidly deteriorating physically, emotionally, and spiritually. I was unable to see my body clearly. When I looked in the mirror, the image I saw was gross, fat, and ugly. What I didn't recognize until years later was that this was the eating disorder's way of trying to slowly kill my mind, body, and spirit. Or in a spiritual sense, I felt like it was Satan's way of keeping me from becoming the strong woman he knew I could become.

I began slipping into a deep depression. My eyes turned a darker shade of blue, and I felt like I was drowning in my negative mind. People in the eating disorder world like to refer to Ed (eating disorders) as the negative mind. Or, if they are Christian, some think of it as Satan's greatest tool to destroy men and women. Take a minute to think about the things your negative mind tells you. Does it say you are too fat, too thin, too tall, too short, or that you have too many zits, you're not pretty enough, you're not smart enough, you're not talented enough, or you're not good enough?

During my eating disorder, I isolated myself from people and things that I once enjoyed. I was so consumed by the eating disorder that I found myself lying to the people I loved the most. I thought by losing weight I would find acceptance and genuine happiness. What I had found instead was that I was far from being the person I really desired to be. I was too deep into the negative mindset to get myself out. I needed help.

THERE IS HOPE

I remember the day I finally began the process of treatment. I was seventeen years old and quickly deteriorating both physically and emotionally. I was blessed with great friends that were able to guide me to professional help. I didn't know how much help I actually needed. A friend of mine took me to the hospital, which began my recovery. I was hospitalized a few times in the next couple of years. The hospital saved my life, but was only a Band-Aid on a much bigger problem. They stabilized me physically, but my mindset was still the same and would eventually relapse.

I have memories of attending a Christian church camp every summer. It was amazing how much better my eating disorder would be for weeks to months following, all because I was making an effort to try and build a relationship with my Heavenly Father. I started believing that I was worth more than the number on a scale. It took me six years to find the right help with the right balance of spirituality, therapy, and dietetics counseling. I couldn't have done it with just one or two of those components. My recovery required all of them working together to heal me physically, mentally, emotionally, and spiritually.

I entered a residential treatment program at the age of nineteen where I was in treatment for five months. It was my last hope. I worked on painful emotional issues and began to understand why I hated my body so much. Eating disorders are not about weight; they are symptoms of self-hatred. The obsession with the body is manifested on the surface as a result of the layers of pain and sorrow buried beneath.

During this time, I learned to rely on my higher power and to allow God to be a constant part of my life. Spirituality and the search for a higher power were instrumental in my recovery process. Identifying a higher power—something greater than we are—is an essential part of the process for anyone wishing to overcome an addiction.

Throughout the next few years, I encountered many physical consequences from my eating disorder. My hair thinned and fell out and many years passed before the healthy texture and thickness returned. My bone density decreased to that of an older woman. Because of this I broke three vertebrae, which continue to cause severe pain in my lower back. Due to a lack of nutrition and over exercise, my heart muscle weakened, and I experienced two near cardiac arrests. Each time I feared it would be the day that I died.

LIFE AFTER AN EATING DISORDER

Recovery is a slow process. There isn't a quick fix to heal all of the complicated layers of this illness. I spent many years fighting the negative thoughts that were so engrained in my mind. There were many days that this battle occurred minute by minute. The fight can be overwhelming, all consuming, and exhausting, but it's worth it! I am not afraid or embarrassed to admit that body image will always be something I am aware of, just like the majority of women in America today. But being aware of it and letting it control your every thought and action are two very different mindsets.

I am now recovered from my eating disorder and have been enjoying my life for the past sixteen years. I have been speaking about my recovery and educating people in schools and youth groups as well as presenting for other organizations and at various conferences. I began studying psychology in school and ended up switching my degree to nursing. I graduated in 2003, and I now work at an inpatient facility for women who struggle with eating disorders. I know that recovery is possible and that there is hope. I love to teach the women who struggle with eating disorders that they can have a life and that they deserve to live and to be loved.

Many of the women I have worked with have tried overcoming their eating disorders with a counselor, a dietician, a prayer, or maybe pure will power. You can try any *one* thing you want, and it will fail every time. You may conquer Ed for the moment or for a small amount of time, but it will come back until you sincerely find yourself.

I found myself through God and through serving others. I couldn't truly love others until I began to love myself. You have to find balance, you have to find peace, you have to gain self-worth, and you have to find your higher power. It doesn't matter if your higher power is God, nature, or the support of a group . . . the important thing is that you find something greater than yourself to motivate, encourage, and inspire you in the positive direction of recovery. Most importantly, you need to establish consistency in recovery.

Today, when I ask myself whether or not it is possible to recover from an eating disorder, I know the answer without a doubt: absolutely, one hundred percent you can recover from an eating disorder! You can live free from the grips and chains of the eating disorder that once ran your life. No more is my every thought bound to the routine of what the negative mind and eating disorder dictates. I have friendships, a husband, and children who love and depend on me every day. Do I struggle sometimes with body image? Sure, who doesn't? But it doesn't run my life anymore; I don't let it. The process by which I got to this point was imperfect, but it has worked for me.

At the beginning, it was hard for me to see some of the benefits of this process. I began being a bit more social, which was uncomfortable at first. My instinct was to stay introverted and reclusive in the comfort of my room, my books, my movies, and my phone. I would only go out if I was ready, whatever that means. It was important for me to not only meet new friends but also hold on to my healthy friends from my past. Limiting contact with friends made in treatment was difficult, but important. It was especially important to me because I needed to get out of my comfort zone.

One of the most valuable lessons I learned from all those years of therapy and treatment was to do the opposite of what the negative mind or Ed tells you to do. I began doing this—sometimes often, sometimes flawlessly. The more I did the opposite, the happier I was. I began to notice that Ed and the negative mind were lessening. I began laughing again. I began paying attention to detail and being more thankful in my life. The importance of prayer was magnified throughout this journey and I no longer felt alone in my efforts to recover.

Although I am very happy and successful in my life right now, I can't help but think about the fact that I wasted what could have possibly been the best years of my life. I should have been going to prom, I should have been laughing with friends, and I should have been applying to colleges. Instead, I was alone, miserable, sad, and depressed. I was slowly torturing myself day in and day out, unaware at the time of the lasting physical impacts my decisions would have on my health for years to come.

One of the difficult things to do throughout the recovery process was to follow doctors' recommendations about staying at a healthy weight, taking calcium supplements, eating well, and finding moderation in exercise. Because I was able to follow their advice, I regained strength in my bones, heart, and body as a whole. Had I chosen to do only the minimum and hold on to a little bit of control, I would not have seen these results and would not have truly recovered from my eating disorder. I know of women who have continued to struggle for many years as a result of trying to do just the minimum requirements for recovery. In turn, they have held onto pieces that have kept them sick and not allowed them to heal their bodies, minds, and spirits.

If I could say one thing to women who may have similar negative thoughts about their body, what they eat, or their self-worth, it would be this: it's not worth it. The destructive behaviors may start out slow and you may think that my story could never be your story. I thought the same thing until I realized I no longer had control of my life. The thoughts turn to actions, and the actions turn into addiction. All of this stems from fear in one way or another—fear of the unknown, feelings of inadequacy, worthlessness, perfectionism, self-hatred, and discouragement. When you are driven by fear, you miss out on life.

You have the opportunity to learn how to deal with these issues in healthy ways. In my opinion, there are very few strong, healthy, and positive female role models in today's media. As women in today's society, we are going to have to rise up, stand a little taller, and strive to be the role models. When we are living in the world and trying to measure up to the standards set by society, we sacrifice peace, joy, and important relationships in our lives. And for what? An obsession with body, exercise, and dieting that in turn will never bring genuine happiness.

Don't be afraid to take a different stand in this world, in your communities, and among your peers. Find moderation in all things and find balance in life. Today if I am hungry for something, I will eat it. I honor my body, and, with a lot of practice, I have learned to listen to it. I truly feel at peace with food. I will never go on a diet again. How peaceful and freeing that sounds!

It's important to remember that eating disorders are not about food or weight; they are the result of much more complicated thoughts, feelings, and behaviors. Dieting does not work; it only causes us to obsess about food and contributes to us hating our bodies.

The choices we make have an impact on those around us. Recovery is about finding moderation in exercise and diet. This, along with a healthy and positive relationship with a higher power, is the way to find peace and joy in this life: a life free from addiction.

You have read this story, and even to me, it sometimes feels like just that—a story. When asked to share about my experience in order to help those who may be struggling, or family and friends who are trying to help someone who is struggling, it was difficult to identify with the person I used to be. I began looking through journals and papers I had written many years ago to try and identify with that person. It saddened me to read them and better understand how broken I had become.

I now have wonderful relationships with my parents, brothers, sisters, friends, and, most importantly, my husband and children. I am proud of the woman I have become, and I continue to strive to become better each day. I will continue to share my experience and love to those who may feel hopeless and helpless in their desire to create a new life. For those of you who are personally struggling with Ed, I want you to know that you can do it! For those of you with loved ones who are struggling, don't give up on them! Recovery isn't a perfect road and there will be bumps along the way, but as long as we strive to be better each day, we are all doing our best, and our best *is* good enough.

resources

RECOMMENDED READING:

- *Intuitive Eating: A Revolutionary Program That Works*, by Evelyn Tribole, M.S., R.D., and Elyse Resch, M.S., R.D., F.A.D.A., C.E.D.R.D.
- *Life Without Ed: How One Woman Declared Independence from Her Eating Disorder and How You Can, Too*, by Jenni Schaefer and Thom Rutledge
- *Goodbye Ed, Hello Me: Recover from Your Eating Disorder and Fall in Love with Life*, by Jenni Schaefer.
- *Almost Anorexic: Is My (or My Loved One's) Relationship with Food a Problem?*, by Jennifer J Thomas and Jenni Schaefer.
- *Bulimia: A Guide to Recovery*, by Lindsay Hall and Leigh Cohn, M.A.T.

RECOMMENDED WEBSITES:

- Center for Change: www.centerforchange.com
- Gurze Books: www.gurze.com
- National Eating Disorder Association (NEDA): www.nationaleating-disorders.org
- American Dietetic Association: www.eatright.org
- Binge Eating Disorder Association: www.bedaonline.org
- Eating Disorder Referral and Information Center: www.edreferral.com
- Something FishyWebsite on Eating Disorders: www.something-fishy.

org
- Anorexics and Bulimics Anonymous (ABA): www.aba12step.org

FOR PROFESSIONALS:

- The International Association of Eating Disorders Professionals Foundation (IADEP) www.iaedp.com

FINANCIAL RESOURCES:

- The Manna Scholarship Fund: The Missing Piece in Eating Disorder Recovery
- FREED Foundation: For Recovery and Elimination of Eating Disorders

about the authors

DEBORAH P. SCHONE is a first-time author and was born and raised in Salt Lake City, Utah. She is one of eight children and has experienced firsthand the pain that comes with the chains of addiction when she lost her youngest brother to a drug overdose and felt the repercussions of similar tragedies. Through rearing her own nine children, three of whom are adopted, she has opened her heart and home to many who have struggled through life-altering choices. She travels abroad to Ethiopia, where she serves the people and helps sponsor several children. She is a photographer and enjoys playing tennis, traveling, and spending time with her husband, Steve, and their children. She and her family currently reside in St. George, Utah.

SHELBY L. EVANS is a licensed substance use disorder counselor who has always taken an interest in helping others. Originally from Washington State, she completed her undergraduate studies at Western Washington University in psychology and communication. She later went on to complete the certification program for substance abuse counseling at the University of Utah. Her perspective is based on professional experience in the field of mental illness. Over a ten-year period, Shelby worked in a therapeutic treatment center for women who struggle with eating disorders and other addictions. She has experience providing both individual and group counseling for those with concurrent eating disorders and substance use disorders. She understands firsthand the heartache and hopelessness that comes with watching a loved one trapped in the cycle of addiction. She has a desire to offer hope and healing to those impacted by these disorders.

Shelby enjoys traveling, golfing, yoga, reading, and spending time with family and friends. She currently lives in Saratoga Springs, Utah, with her husband and daughter.

about familius

Welcome to a place where mothers are celebrated, not compared. Where heart is at the center of our families, and family at the center of our homes. Where boo boos are still kissed, cake beaters are still licked, and mistakes are still okay. Welcome to a place where books—and family— are beautiful. Familius: a book publisher dedicated to helping families be happy.

Visit Our Website: www.familius.com

Our website is a different kind of place. Get inspired, read articles, discover books, watch videos, connect with our family experts, download books and apps and audiobooks, and along the way, discover how values and happy family life go together.

Join Our Family

There are lots of ways to connect with us! Subscribe to our newsletters at www.familius.com to receive uplifting daily inspiration, essays from our Pater Familius, a free ebook every month, and the first word on special discounts and Familius news.

Become an Expert

Familius authors and other established writers interested in helping families be happy are invited to join our family and contribute online content. If you have something important to say on the family, join our expert community by applying at:

www.familius.com/apply-to-become-a-familius-expert

Get Bulk Discounts

If you feel a few friends and family might benefit from what you've read, let us know and we'll be happy to provide you with quantity discounts. Simply email us at specialorders@familius.com.

Website: www.familius.com

Facebook: www.facebook.com/paterfamilius

Twitter: @familiustalk, @paterfamilius1

Pinterest: www.pinterest.com/familius

The most important work

you ever do will be within the

walls of your own home.

CPSIA information can be obtained at www.ICGtesting.com
Printed in the USA
BVOW07s1902160614

356377BV00003B/35/P